DATE DUE

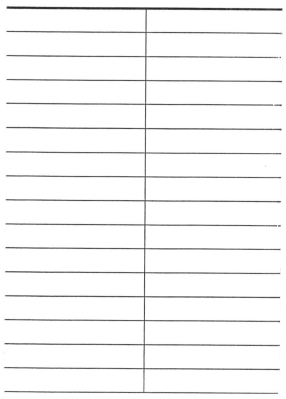

ANNUS HORRIBILIS

LATIN FOR EVERYDAY LIFE

ANNUS HORRIBILIS

LATIN FOR EVERYDAY LIFE

Mark Walker

Non scholae sed vitae discimus
(Seneca)

First published 2007

Reprinted in 2008 by The History Press

The History Press
The Mill, Brimscombe Port,
Stroud, Gloucestershire, GL5 2QG
www.thehistorypress.co.uk

British Library Cataloguing in Publication Data.
A catalogue record for this book is available from the British Library.

ISBN 978 0 7524 4284 6

ry Press

1

ABOUT THE AUTHOR

Mark Walker gained his own Latin qualifications as an adult, an experience which inspired him to create his own bespoke Latin course specifically for adult learners. He currently teaches that course, *Latin for Everyday Life*, via Buckinghamshire's Adult Education programme.

Mark holds a degree in Philosophy from Durham University, and is currently studying for an MA in Classics with Lampeter University, building on the abiding love of Classical history and literature that has informed his work in recent years. In 2004, Mark set up Pineapple Publications (www.pineapplepubs.co.uk) to publish his first novel *Amida*, an ambitious historical epic set in the declining years of the Roman Empire.

During his previous career in publishing and journalism, Mark wrote, edited and contributed to many books, magazines, newspapers and internet sites. In the mid-1990s he was the editor of the *Gramophone Film Music* and *Musicals Good CD Guides*, and has written extensively about both music and movies.

CONTENTS

ACKNOWLEDGEMENTS

I would like to thank all the authors of the books mentioned in the *Recommended reading* boxes at the end of each chapter, as well as the writers of innumerable articles and web pages that I have also consulted concerning points of grammar or interpretation. Any errors are solely mine.

INTRODUCTION

Why study Latin?

It is often said that Latin is a dead language. But reports of its death have been wildly exaggerated. Latin is alive and well and thriving all around us. It is still widely used in

Medicine	Philosophy	Law
Science	The Church	Music

Latin is also useful for:

- Historians and genealogists
- Gardeners
- Students of other European languages
- Writers who wish to improve their English grammar and vocabulary
- Readers of English literature
- Music lovers
- Classicists and all those fascinated by the Ancient World, naturally

to name just a few areas of our professional and personal lives where we routinely find Latin. Indeed, though estimates vary, it is generally reckoned that some *60 per cent* of our day-to-day English vocabulary is derived either directly or indirectly from Latin. We also use many Latin words and phrases unaltered and untranslated in everyday life (e.g. *ad hoc, quid pro quo, caveat emptor, ad nauseam* etc.), not to mention Latin abbreviations (e.g. *e.g., q.v., i.e., etc.,* etc.). Latin is to be found everywhere in everyday life, from football team mottoes to rock bands (*Status Quo, Procul Harum*) to political parties (*Veritas*).

Anyone interested in good English – both spoken and written – will find Latin invaluable as a reference source for grammatical correctness in our own language. Learn a little Latin and you'll never get your possessives and plurals mixed up, you'll never confuse 'who' with 'whom', and you'll never boldly go to split an infinitive again!

The Classical Latin authors exercised a formative influence on English writers, and hence on the development of English literature generally. Ovid's *Metamorphoses* was Shakespeare's favourite book; Milton wrote *Paradise Lost* as a Christian epic in the manner of Virgil's *Aeneid*. The *King James Bible* itself, one of the pillars of the English language, is based on the Latin Vulgate of St Jerome. Latinity, the style and mannerisms of Latin authors, runs deep in our literature.

Latin is also the basis of the Romance languages – French, Spanish, Portuguese and Italian (also Romanian) – so-called since they are all direct descendants of Latin, the 'Roman' language, and share much similar grammar and vocabulary both with their parent and among themselves. Hence, knowing some Latin makes learning modern languages easier.

About this book

This book came about as a result of my teaching an evening class in Latin for adult beginners. It was apparent to me that the traditional Latin courses on offer were not ideally suited to the needs of my mature students. So I decided to create a new one just for them.

Most Latin textbooks are for school use and even the few intended for adults focus almost exclusively on the art of reading literary Latin texts from the Classical age. Of course, there's nothing at all wrong with reading Latin literature; quite the contrary, it's an immensely rewarding experience. However, it takes years of hard work before a student can begin to appreciate the *Aeneid* or the poems of Horace or any of the other wonderful literary relics of Ancient Rome.

Between work and family and sundry other commitments, the adults who attend my evening classes simply don't have the time for such studying; nor do they necessarily have the desire either. *Annus Horribilis: Latin for Everyday Life* is designed specifically for such people. It's not a shortcut to proficiency in the language but its professed goal throughout is to apply this 'theoretical' knowledge to the Latin we all encounter 'out there' in the world rather than just in books. In other words, this is a course in Applied Latin.

Used in conjunction with a good dictionary, this book will provide even Latin beginners with a firm basis for further study. Once you get bitten by the Latin bug, it's hard to stop. From successfully translating epitaphs and inscriptions it's only a short step to reading real Latin authors – a worthwhile and worthy goal for all Latinists. If you have absorbed all the lessons in this book, the transition should be a painless one.

How to use this book

In the first eight chapters only single words or very short sentences – familiar phrases, abbreviations, mottoes etc. – are under consideration. Readers who are just starting their Latin studies should naturally begin at the beginning. Thereafter, from Chapter 9 onwards, the Latin becomes more ambitious as we turn our attention to full-length texts: from the complete Latin Mass to Roman Inscriptions and Latin Epitaphs.

Latin novices should turn to the Appendix at the end of this book for a very brief introduction to Latin grammar: the Glossary especially is designed to be consulted whenever an unfamiliar term crops up in the main chapters. Thereafter, a good dictionary, such as one of those recommended below, and a more thorough guide to Latin grammar will be invaluable for all and any wishing to have a go at making their own translations of the texts.

To help you along with your own translating attempts, I provide full grammatical notes for each passage. At the end of the book you will find my own English versions of all the texts encountered in Chapters 9 to 15.

Recommended reference books:

Latin-English, English-Latin Dictionary (Cassell)
  comes in either a Standard or Concise edition, both excellent.

Lewis & Short's *Latin Dictionary* (OUP)
  the heavyweight (literally!) among Latin dictionaries.

501 Latin Verbs (Barron's)
  an invaluable study aid.

Latin Grammar (OUP)
  a handy paperback companion.

Kennedy's *Revised Latin Primer* (Longman)
  a more detailed survey of grammar.

CHAPTER 1

A BRIEF HISTORY OF LATIN

Have you ever done something *ad hoc* or on a *quid pro quo* basis? Do you get paid *per annum* or *pro rata*? Have you ever been caught *in flagrante* and been in need of an *alibi*, an *alias* or an *alter ego*?

If you think you don't know any Latin, think again. In fact, though you might not realise it yet, you already know thousands of Latin words. Here are just a few them:

Actor	Exit
Agenda	Insomnia
Alibi	Interim
Alias	Propaganda
Audio	Referendum
Circus	Tandem
Curriculum	Tedium
Data	Trivia
Decorum	Ultimatum
Doctor	Video

These are all real Latin words that any ancient Roman would recognise. And you thought learning Latin was going to be tough!

The reason this book is subtitled *Latin for Everyday Life* – with the emphasis on *Everyday* – is because there really is that much Latin in modern English. But why should our language, so remote in time from that of Ancient Rome, contain great chunks of Latin? In order to answer that question a quick sketch of Latin history is called for. That's the purpose of this chapter, before we move on to Chapter 2 and actually start learning some Latin. So here goes.

A VERY BRIEF HISTORY OF LATIN

Latin was originally the dialect of the region of Italy called Latium (modern Lazio), but as a result of the military and political

Virgil (70-19 B.C.)

Publius Vergilius Maro was arguably the finest exponent of the Latin language. His most famous work is *The Aeneid*, a national Roman epic modelled on both Homer's *Iliad* and *Odyssey*, and rivalling both.

dominance of Rome it soon spread throughout Italy and then to all the provinces of the Roman Empire, right round the Mediterranean into the Middle East and Africa and as far north as Hadrian's Wall. Throughout this vast geographical area, Latin was the language of law, administration, commerce and literature.

Although in the East it didn't entirely displace Greek, which was already well established as the *lingua franca* (literally 'Frankish language') of that region, in the Western Empire Latin was rapidly adopted as the principal language of the Iberian Peninsula (Spain and Portugal) and Gaul (France and Belgium). This is the origin of the so-called 'Romance' languages as we know them today: 'Roman' was what people in these territories called their spoken tongue, whereas 'Latin' gradually came to be reserved for the more formal written language – though no distinction was made between the two for many centuries.

To illustrate the process of change from Latin to the Romance languages, just take a look at the most common verb in any language, 'to be' – *esse* in Latin. This is *essere* in Italian, *ser* in Spanish, and *être* in French. In the table below it is conjugated in Latin then Italian, Spanish and French:

Latin	Italian	Spanish	French
sum	sono	soy	je suis
es	sei	eres	tu es
est	é	es	il/elle/on est
sumus	siamo	somos	nous sommes
estis	siete	sois	vous êtres
sunt	sono	son	ils/elles sont

The family resemblance is clear at a glance. (It's worth noting in passing that both Italian and Spanish can dispense with the personal pronouns 'I', 'You' etc. just as Latin does.)

By contrast, 'to be' in English conjugates like this:

> I am
> you are
> he/she/it is
> we are
> you are
> they are

As we've already noted, the Romance languages developed from the spoken form of Latin – the *sermo cotidianus* or daily speech – which was not necessarily the same as the written form that has come down to us in the remnants of Latin literature. Take, for example, the Latin word for horse: this is *equus* in literary Latin. Compare this with the Romance language words for 'horse':

Latin	Italian	Spanish	French
Equus	Cavallo	Caballo	Cheval

Clearly, *equus* is not the source word. But Latin has another word for 'horse', a slang word meaning 'pack-horse' or 'nag': *caballus*. This slang word was presumably the one in common use on the streets of Rome, hence the one that found its way into the spoken Romance languages, while *equus* only survived in polite literature. English gets 'chivalry', 'cavalry' and 'cavalier' from *caballus*, via French, but 'equine' and 'equestrian' from Latin.

After the fall of the Western Roman Empire, Latin continued to be the official language of the Catholic Church (in the Byzantine territories of the East, Greek was still used). Christian Latin thus spread into Germany and Scandinavia and was reintroduced to the British Isles where it had all but disappeared following the withdrawal of Roman forces. This Church Latin, exemplified by Jerome's Vulgate Bible (Chapter 9), had a somewhat different syntax and vocabulary to Classical Latin, although Christian scholars still studied pagan authors such as Virgil.

Classical Latin itself was rediscovered by secular Europe during the Renaissance of the fourteenth and fifteenth centuries, when the writings of Roman authors such as Cicero and Seneca began to be widely circulated and proved highly influential in the new climate

Erasmus (c.1469-1536)

Dutch Latin scholar Gerhard Gerhards (Erasmus) not only produced editions of numerous Classical Latin texts by Pliny and Seneca among others, he also wrote copiously in Latin about Latin. His most famous work is *Moriae Encomium* ('In Praise of Folly'), published in 1511.

of open-minded intellectual curiosity. Throughout Europe, Latin became the language of science and scholarship, a fact that greatly facilitated the dissemination of learning. For example, Swedish scientist Carl Linnaeus (1707-1778) used Latin for his system of biological classification (Chapter 6); because all his scientific peers understood Latin, his system was quickly taken up by botanists and biologists everywhere, regardless of their native tongue.

Thus Latin in its *spoken* form has evolved into the Romance languages of today; in its *written* form, however, it was preserved largely unchanged by the Church and was then taken up by secular scholars during and after the Renaissance.

LATIN IN ENGLISH

Although Latin was introduced to Britain by the Roman conquest in the mid-first century A.D., it did not long survive the collapse of the Western Empire in the fifth century: an indication that it had failed to displace the native languages in the British Isles, as had happened elsewhere. In the centuries that followed, the Church and its missionaries gradually reintroduced Latin to Britain. But in the meantime a native literary tradition had begun to flourish, most famously exemplified by the Anglo-Saxon epic *Beowulf* which was probably composed in the eighth century, a time when, according to the Venerable Bede, there were five languages spoken in Britain ...

> ... *Anglorum videlicet, Brettonum, Scottorum, Pictorum et Latinorum, quae meditatione Scripturarum ceteris omnibus est facta communis*

> ... namely those of the Angles, the Bretons, the Scots [i.e. the Irish], the Picts and the Latins, which latter language is shared among all the other races for contemplation of the Scriptures

Bede (c.672/3-735)

The Venerable Bede was a Northumbrian monk and scholar who wrote elegant, precise Latin in a simpler, more direct style than his Classical predecessors. His *Historia Ecclesiastica* earned him the title 'Father of English History', since it recounts the major events in British history from the Roman occupation to his own time. The book is also full of vivid and dramatic stories, making it an excellent if overlooked example of Latin prose.

Later, King Alfred (871-899) strived to establish a distinctly English literary culture after the depredations of the Vikings had all but wiped out scholarly communities in many regions. But the arrival of William the Conqueror in 1066 achieved what the Vikings had failed to do: native British literature was exterminated.

As a result of the Norman conquest, the nascent English language was forced to abandon its literary pretensions, becoming nothing but a poor spoken relation to French, the language of the conquering dynasty for centuries afterwards. Naturally all official business in Norman England was now conducted in Latin.

Gradually as the conquerors became naturalised English re-emerged, only now in a much altered form. Thanks to the Normans and their mix of spoken French and written Latin, English had absorbed a huge influx of Latin and Latin-derived words, a process that was greatly to its benefit. This revitalised English showed its new expressive power in the works of Chaucer and Spenser and, ultimately, of Shakespeare.

After the Renaissance, English also took in many words directly from Latin as deliberate borrowings when new terms were needed for technical and scientific developments. This process is still ongoing: recent examples include 'satellite', from the word *satelles* (*satellitis* in the genitive case) meaning 'attendant' or 'bodyguard' and the ubiquitous 'video', which is simply 'I see', the first person singular of the Latin verb *videre*.

Partly as a result of historical accident and partly by design, then, modern English is a distinct oddity among European languages: it belongs to the same Germanic family as those of Scandinavia and Germany, but it has far more Latin-derived words than German-derived ones. This mixed heritage provides English with a fertile source of synonyms: for example, we can choose between the Germanic 'come' and the Latin-derived 'arrive'; or we can say 'brotherly', from the Germanic 'brother' (German *brüder*), but we can also say 'fraternal', from the Latin *frater*. Modern English owes much of its worldwide success to its Latin inheritance.

Recommended reading:

T. Janson   *A Natural History of Latin*
Oxford University Press
An accessible survey of the development of Latin from its earliest times to the present day.

Virgil (trans. Fitzgerald)   *The Aeneid*
Everyman's Library
A splendid English translation that captures the majesty of Virgil's stately Latin hexameters.

Bede (ed. Garforth)   *Historia Ecclesiastica* (selections)
Bolchazy-Carducci
For those with enough Latin, F.W. Garforth's selection from Bede includes historical background, illustrations and explanatory notes on the text.

CHAPTER 2

CONVERSATIONAL LATIN

Cicero (106-43 B.C.)

Marcus Tullius Cicero was one of the greatest Roman orators and statesmen. Many of his speeches for the law courts and the Senate have been preserved. These are in the grandest style of Latin oratory, a far cry from the *sermo cotidianus*, the daily speech of everyday Romans. But he also left many letters, addressed to his friend Atticus or to members of his family (including his freedman Tiro). These are far more chatty in tone, giving us a unique portrait of Cicero the man rather than the statesman of his speeches.

When inspecting inscriptions in stone or reading literary quotations it's easy to forget that Latin was once a vehicle for *conversation* – just like any modern language. All the written remains of old Latin added together represent only a fraction of that 'real' Latin, the language now lost to us because it is no longer spoken. True, there is the Latin of the Catholic Church which, even in the twenty-first century, occasionally gets a public airing when Popes are inaugurated or laid to rest, but such Church Latin (Chapter 9) has both a distinct pronunciation and a distinct vocabulary – when we think of 'proper' Latin, we naturally think of how Cicero or Julius Caesar might have talked.

Classical Latin, then, means the language spoken from, roughly, the beginning of the first century B.C. through to the end of the first century A.D. This was the period of Latin's literary greatness, from the comedies of Plautus and Terence to the late, great work of the historian Tacitus.

PRONOUNCING THE LATIN ALPHABET

A B C D E F G H I K L M N O P Q R S T V (X Y Z)

- I and V (i and v) serve both as vowels *and* consonants. They are consonants when they appear *before a vowel*, otherwise they are vowels
- J/j is unknown in Classical Latin, it was invented later to represent consonantal-i (a 'j' is just 'i' with a curl at the base)
- K is only found in *Kalendae* and a few archaic words, otherwise C is used
- V is consonantal-u, not a separate consonant
- W does not exist (sounds the same as consonantal-u)
- X, Y, Z were only used in words borrowed from Greek (e.g. Xenophon, Zeno)

It's cheering to note that most letters of the Latin alphabet are pronounced in much the same way as English – we did inherit our alphabet from the Romans after all. Sadly Julius Caesar didn't leave behind any recordings of his speeches, so how do we know how he spoke? Evidence comes from a variety of sources. Classical Latin writers on language and grammar such as Varro and Quintillian discuss the subject in their books. Furthermore, analysis of Latin poetry, with its emphasis on long or short vowels and heavy or light syllable quantities, reveals much about how Roman writers expected their words to sound when read aloud. The main points to note are:

1. *Consonants*

- c is always hard as in *cat*, never soft as in *cider*. Hence, *Caesar* would have been pronounced *Kaesar*, whence German *Kaiser* and Russian *Tsar*
- g is always hard as in *get*, never soft as in *gentle*
- consonantal-i sounds like *y* as in *yet*
- n before c, g, or qu is like *ng* in *sing*
- r is always rolled
- t is always hard as in *ten*, never soft *sh* as in *potion*
- v is consonantal-u and is always *w* as in *wall*, not *v* as in *very*. Hence, Caesar's famous saying *Veni, vidi, vici* ('I came, I saw, I conquered') is pronounced *Wayny, weedy, weeky*

Doubled consonants are pronounced separately, as strictly speaking should *ch*, *th*, *ph*:

- cc   like *book-case*
- ch   like *ink-horn*, not *chain*
- th   like *hot-house*, not *this*
- ph   like *tap-house*, not *f* as in *philosophy*

(in practice it sounds odd to say *p-hil-oso-p-hia*, so the normal English pronunciation is acceptable for such familiar words)

2. *Diphthongs* (two vowels pronounced as one):

- ai   as in *aisle*
- au   ou as in *house*
- ei   as in *rein*
- eu   e-oo all in one breath
- oe   oi as in *toil*
- ui   like *we*

3. *Vowels*

Vowels can either be short or long depending on certain conventions and context, for example *femina* (nominative case) has a short 'a' as in 'cat', but *femina* (ablative case) has a long 'a' as in 'father'. Thus the difference between the nominative and ablative form of the word would have been clear to a Roman thanks to this distinct pronunciation, though we who usually deal only with written Latin are easily confused!

CONVERSATIONAL LATIN

In case you meet an ancient Roman, a Pope, or a fellow Latin student:

1. *Saying 'Hello'*

    salve! (if addressing just one person)
    salvete! (if addressing more than one person)

- *salve* literally means: 'Be well!'. Remember that 'v' is pronounced 'w': *sal-way*
- these are the imperative forms of the verb *salveo, salvere*, 'be well/in good health'
- can also be used to say farewell

or

> *ave*! (singular)
> *avete*! (plural)

This means 'Hail!' as in:
- *ave atque vale*, 'Hail and farewell' (from a poem by Catullus)
- *ave Caesar! morituri te salutant*, 'Hail, Caesar, those about to die salute you' (gladiators' salute)
- *Ave Maria gratia plena*, 'Hail Mary full of grace' (hymn)
- *ave* and *avete* are the imperative forms of the verb *aveo, avere*, 'fare well'

or

> *salvus sis* (addressing a man)
> *salva sis* (addressing a woman)

- literally means: 'May you be well'
- *sis* is the subjunctive (expressing a wish or desire) form of the verb *sum, esse* ('to be')

2. Asking & Saying Your Name

> Q: *quid nomen est tibi*?
> A: *nomen est mihi* ...

> 'What's your name?'
> 'My name is ...'

- *tibi* and *mihi* are dative case of the personal pronouns *ego* ('I') and *tu* ('you'). Literally the Latin means 'What name is there to you?' 'There is a name to me ...' i.e. 'What name do you have/possess?' 'I have/possess the name ...'

- *nomen*, genitive case *nominis*, from which we get the English words 'nominate', 'nominal' and 'nomenclature' (a system of names)

3. Saying 'Goodbye'

> *vale*! (singular)
> *valete*! (plural)

- literally means: 'Be strong!'
- these are the imperative forms of the verb *valeo, valere*

bonum vesperum	'Good evening'
bonam noctem	'Good night'

- *bonum* and *bonam* are the same word, two forms of the accusative case of the adjective *bonus, -a, -um*. Because *vesper, vesperis*, 'evening', is masculine gender, accusative case, the adjective must also be masculine accusative: *bonum*. But *nox, noctis*, 'night' (English 'nocturnal') is feminine accusative, so the adjective also becomes feminine accusative: *bonam*.

4. Asking 'How are you?'

ut vales?	'Are you well/strong?'
quid agis?	'What are you doing?'

Possible replies:

optime, et tu	'Very well (literally: best) and you?'
valeo	'I am well'
bene maneo	'I remain well'
non male	'Not bad'
satis bene	'Well enough'
non ita bene	'Not so well'
pessime	'Terrible' (literally: 'worst')

5. 'Thanks'

> *gratias ago tibi* (singular) literally: 'I give thanks to you'
> *gratias ago vobis* (plural)

- *tibi*, meaning 'to you' (singular) is the dative case of *tu*, 'you' (singular); *vobis*, meaning 'to you' (plural) is the dative case of *vos*, 'you' (plural)
- *gratias*, 'thanks', is accusative plural of *gratia*, 'favour', 'kindness' (English 'grace')
- n.b. similarity with modern Italian *grazie*, Spanish *gracias*

6. 'Yes' and 'No'

Oddly, the Romans didn't have words exactly corresponding to our 'yes' and 'no'. Here are some they used instead:

Expressions meaning 'yes':

est	'it is'
ita est	'it is so'
etiam	'even'
ita	'thus'
ita vero	'thus indeed'
sane	'certainly'
certe	'surely'
recte	'correctly'

Expressions meaning 'no':

non	'not'
non ita	'not so'
minime	'indeed not' (literally: 'least')

Frequently, Romans would simply affirm or negate the question by repetition, e.g.

> Q. *venitne pater tuus?* 'Is your father coming?'
> A. *venit* 'He is coming'

7. Exclamations!

Finally, when you need to give vent to your feelings, try a few of these:

malum	'damn!' (literally: 'a bad thing')
insanum bonum	'damned good!' (literally: 'a crazy good thing')
euge	'well done!'
eheu	'alas!'
ecastor/edepol	'by Castor!' / 'by Pollux!'
hercule/hercle/mehercule/mehercle	
	'by Hercules!'
pro Iuppiter	'by Jupiter!'
pro di immortales	'by the immortal gods!'
di te ament	'(may the gods) bless you'
di te perdant	'damn you!' (literally: 'may the gods destroy you')

Recommended reading:

W.S. Allen   *Vox Latina*
                 Cambridge University Press
A scholarly survey of the evidence for the correct pronunciation of Classical Latin.

J.C. Traupman   *Conversational Latin for Oral Proficiency*
                 Bolchazy-Carducci
An enjoyable series of Latin dialogues for modern situations, from asking about the weather to clothes shopping to visiting the zoo.

CHAPTER 3

FAMILIAR LATIN PHRASES

Take a look at this list of Latin phrases. You are sure to know at least some of them, and many of the rest will have a familiar ring even if you're not certain what they mean:

ad nauseam	*memento mori*
quid pro quo	*ne plus ultra*
caveat emptor	*in flagrante delicto*
habeas corpus	*in loco parentis*
inter alia	*post mortem*
annus horribilis	*in situ*
carpe diem	*compos mentis*
magnum opus	*sine qua non*
cave canem	*alter ego*
in toto	*ad hoc*
alma mater	*bona fide*

There are many hundreds of such expressions still in more or less common use in English. They are relics of the time when ordinary discourse in law, medicine, the sciences and many other professions was conducted in Latin. Most of them came into English in medieval times, though some are quotations from Classical authors. Take a moment to translate those expressions which you do know and you will find that either (a) the English is just a literal translation adding nothing to an expression distinguished by venerable historical usage, or (b) the English produces a clumsy circumlocution (good Latin-derived word, that) where the original is neat and tidy. You will find all these

> **Horace** (65-27 B.C.)
>
> Quintus Horatius Flaccus was a member of the same literary circle as Virgil. In his poems he coined many phrases still quoted, such as *carpe diem* ('seize the day') and *dulce et decorum est pro patria mori* ('It is sweet and fitting to die for one's country').

phrases translated at the end of the chapter. But first, let's examine some in more detail:

ad hoc

An excellent example of why such Latin phrases remain in common parlance, *ad hoc* literally means 'to this'. But the literal rendering does no justice to the many contexts in which this useful little phrase occurs: an *ad hoc* committee meeting, an *ad hoc* repair to my broken lawnmower, 'the plan was a bit *ad hoc* but it worked'. What we mean is something impromptu, something done for a particular purpose and no other. See what I mean about clumsy English circumlocutions. Better simply to say *ad hoc*.

Like many other 'everyday Latin' expressions, *ad hoc* is a prepositional phrase consisting of two parts: the preposition *ad* plus another word, *hoc*, in the accusative case. *ad nauseam* in the list above is another example of the same construction, adding the accusative of *nausea* ('sickness') to the preposition *ad*, the basic meaning of which is 'to, towards'. So the phrase means 'To the point of sickness'. Other examples include:

ad infinitum	'To infinity', 'endlessly'
ad lib. (*ad libitum*)	literally: 'Towards being pleased', so 'as one pleases', 'freely' (in performance, an improvisation)
ad absurdum	'To the point of absurdity'
ad hominem	'Towards/concerning the man' (in legal terms an argument directed at a person's character rather than their actions)

As you can see, that little word *ad* has many shades of meaning. Which is why it has proved indispensable in English.

alma mater

Literally 'nourishing mother', in the old-fashioned sense of a wet-nurse, i.e. not the biological mother but the one from whom an infant received its first nourishment (in centuries past, well-to-do mothers would never have dreamt of suckling their own children – that was a job for the hired help). Both the English and Latin phrases have come to be employed metaphorically, the Latin being specifically applied to the institution – usually a University – in which a person received their intellectual nourishment.

Mater is the noun, in the nominative case (genitive singular *matris*), which provides English with not only 'maternal' but also 'matricide', the latter a compound from the stem *matri-* plus verb *cado, cadere* (*cecidi* in the perfect tense) – 'kill'. The adjective *alma* is the feminine form, agreeing with *mater*: the phrase's non-existent masculine equivalent thus would be *almus pater*.

annus horribilis

This is an easy one, 'a horrible year', famously used by Queen Elizabeth II to describe a particularly tumultuous year in the House of Windsor (1992). Latin *annus*, 'year', gives us English 'annual', and if you're lucky an 'annuity'. In the ablative case *annus* expresses 'the year in which', as in *A.D.* – *Anno Domini* – 'in the year of the Lord', i.e. the date as reckoned from the birth of Jesus.

The phrase *annus horribilis* is an adaptation of the apparently more optimistic *annus mirabilis*, 'a wonderful year'. But only apparently optimistic, because the adjective *mirabilis* means 'wonderful' in the original sense of something to be wondered at, that is something astonishing or extraordinary. Not all such things are necessarily good – Dryden uses the phrase *annus mirabilis* to describe 1666, the year of the Great Fire of London.

The verb from which the adjective *mirabilis* is derived, *miror* ('wonder at', 'be astonished'), also gives us the neuter noun *miraculum*, 'a wonderful thing', hence English 'miracle'.

bona fide

An adjectival phrase used to describe how something is done, 'in good faith'. Both the adjective *bona* and the noun *fide* are in the ablative case. Put them both in the nominative case, singular, and we get *bona fides* – simply 'good faith'. We often pluralise this latter phrase in English when we talk about someone 'having established their *bona fides*' – though nominative plural of *bona* is actually *bonae*.

A Latin speaker would distinguish between *bona* nominative and *bona* ablative because the latter has a long 'a' – *bonā* (see

Chapter 2). So pronounce *bona fides* 'bon-a fee-days', but *bona fide* as 'bon-ah feeday' (note the 'o' is short as in 'dog', unlike the long 'o' in English 'bonus').

caveat emptor

Latin uses the subjunctive to express, among other things, a wish or a warning, as in the phrase *caveat emptor*, 'Let/May the buyer beware!' (a phrase well worth bearing in mind when shopping online). A 'caveat' in English, therefore, is a word of caution.

The dictionary form of the verb that gives us *caveat* is *caveo, cavere*, from which we also get the imperative singular *cave*, as in *cave canem*, 'Beware of the dog!' This is a genuine Roman phrase, famously found inscribed on a mosaic 'doormat' outside the entrance to one of the houses in Pompeii.

Note that the imperative is typically used in the second person (either singular or plural), i.e. 'You – beware of the dog'. Whereas the subjunctive generally occurs in the third person, e.g. *Floreat*, 'May it flourish!' or *Fiat lux*, 'Let there be light!'

in situ
in toto

'In its place' – with the implication that it is the original and proper place – and 'in its entirety', are two small prepositional phrases with *in* + the ablative case. Here *in* really does mean 'in' (whereas *in* + the accusative case means 'into' as in *in medias res*, 'into the midst of things').

The noun *situs*, 'place' (English 'site'), is fourth declension, easily remembered when we see the ablative singular *situ*: other examples of fourth declension nouns are *manus*, 'hand' (English 'manual') and *genu*, 'knee' (as in 'genuflect' – a compound with the verb *flecto, flectere*, 'bend'). Contrast *totus*, 'whole' (English 'total'), which is a first-second declension adjective, masculine in this form, whose ablative is therefore *toto* (not to be confused with Dorothy's dog Toto).

inter alia

Simply, 'among other things' as in, 'We discussed at the board meeting, *inter alia*, the subject of your pay rise'. *Inter* along with its counterpart *intra* is one of those little Latin prepositions (*post, pro* and *per* are other examples – *post mortem*, *pro rata* and *per se*) that continually crop up in English. *Inter* means 'among' or 'between' whereas *intra* means 'within': hence the modern distinction that most office workers will know well between the Internet (the place to do your shopping during lunch) and the Intranet (the place where all that dull corporate stuff can be found).

Both prepositions are followed by a word in the accusative case, here *alia* being the neuter plural accusative of another familiar word, *alius*, 'other' or 'another'. Since the word is neuter 'other *things*' is quite correct.

Alius is also the source of another familiar word, *alias* – which is its adverbial form meaning, 'at another time'. The little set phrase *alius alias* means 'one person at one time, another person at another time' (how compact Latin is!), hence our English sense of someone with an *alias*.

memento mori

A *memento* in English is a keepsake, something of which memories are made: but in Latin it's an imperative, that is a command to 'remember!' – though note such a command, unlike regular imperatives, implies futurity: 'remember x in the future'. The verb is the deponent *memini*, 'I remember' (infinitive *meminisse*), a so-called 'defective' verb since it has no present tense conjugation: *memini* is the perfect tense form, though its meaning is present tense and *memento* is the imperative (plural *mementote!*).

Mori is the infinitive form of another deponent verb, *morior*, 'I die' (deponents like *memini* and *morior* look passive but are active in meaning). Hence *memento mori* is literally the injunction, 'remember to die!', or better, 'remember you are going to die'. In English the phrase is a reminder of our own mortality, often applied to an object such as a skull decoration on a tombstone.

ne plus ultra

The acme, the highest, that beyond which there is nothing greater. *Ne* is a Latin negative which properly takes a verb in the subjunctive, but here it simply negates *plus*, 'more' (the plural of which is *plures*, giving English 'plural'), while *ultra* is, you've guessed it, 'beyond': literally the phrase is 'no more beyond'.

quid pro quo

This is a good case study of how a preposition changes the inflection of the word it qualifies. *Quid*, 'something', and *quo* are the same word, but the intervention of *pro* changes *quid* into *quo* – from the nominative to the ablative case. The basic meaning of *pro* is 'for, on behalf of' though like *ad* it has a variety of nuances. So the phrase's simplest interpretation is 'something for something', by which we mean 'You scratch my back I'll scratch yours', 'tit for tat'.

Don't however confuse this *quo* with another very familiar use of *quo* in the phrase *status quo ante*, 'the state in which it was before', often simply *status quo*, 'the state in which', that is something remaining in its current state, unchanging (like, say, a certain rock band who built a whole career on a very specific 12-bar shuffle rhythm). Latin has quite a few of these pitfalls. Such little words are sent to try us.

FAMILIAR PHRASES TRANSLATED

ad nauseam	To the point of sickness
quid pro quo	Something for something, an exchange of favours
caveat emptor	Let the buyer beware!
habeas corpus	You must produce the body (see Chapter 8)
inter alia	Among other things
annus horribilis	A horrible year
carpe diem	Seize (literally: pluck) the day!
magnum opus	A great work
cave canem	Beware of the dog!
in toto	In its entirety
alma mater	Nourishing mother
memento mori	Remember that you will die
ne plus ultra	'No more beyond', i.e. the very best
in flagrante delicto	'In a blazing crime', i.e. caught red-handed (see Chapter 8)
in loco parentis	In place of the parent, a parental substitute
post mortem	After death

in situ	In its place
compos mentis	Sound of mind
sine qua non	'Without which not', i.e. indispensable
alter ego	Another self
ad hoc	For a particular purpose
bona fide	In good faith

Recommended reading:

J. Morwood (ed.)   *A Dictionary of Latin Words and Phrases*
Oxford University Press
Does exactly what it says on the cover.

CHAPTER 4

ACRONYMS & ABBREVIATIONS

Lots of Latin phrases in English are actually more familiar as acronyms or abbreviations, so much so that many of us are either unaware that such things as *e.g.* or *etc.* are Latin at all, or we don't really know what they are abbreviations of. So in this chapter we'll take a look at some everyday examples (there are plenty more), handily divided into these categories:

- Sepulchral abbreviations
- Academic abbreviations
- Literary abbreviations
- Miscellaneous

Each list is followed by notes on points of interest.

1. Sepulchral abbreviations

These are the kind frequently seen on tombstones and epitaphs in churches or cathedrals. They usually employ a quite distinct set of abbreviations from those found in actual ancient Roman inscriptions – but for now we'll save the Roman ones for study in Chapter 14 and we'll revisit the subject of Church inscriptions in more detail in Chapter 15.

The reason for all these mysterious letters, either ancient or (relatively) modern, is obvious: when carving in stone it saves space as well as time and money to shorten certain set phrases instead of spelling them out in full and back in the days when both churchgoing and a Classical education were more commonplace than now, most readers would reasonably have been expected to understand such a Stygian shorthand.

A.D.	*Anno Domini*	In the year of the Lord
A.S.	*Anno Salutis*	In the year of Salvation

D.S.P.	*decessit sine prole*	Died without issue
D.V.	*Deo volente*	God willing
H.I.S. or H.J.S.	*hic iacet/jacet sepultus*	Here lies buried
H.M.	*hoc monumentum*	This monument
H.S.E.	*hic sepultus est*	Here is buried
I.N.R.I.	*Iesus Nazarenus Rex Iudaeorum*	Jesus of Nazareth, King of the Jews
M.S.	*memoriae sacrum*	Sacred to the memory
ob.	*obiit*	He/she died
R.I.P.	*requiescat in pace*	May he/she rest in peace

A.D.

In Latin, the ablative case is used to express the time *when* something is happening, as in *Anno Domini* – 'in the year [ablative] of the Lord [genitive]'. *Dominus* (second declension) in Classical Latin means 'master' as in the master of the house – the lady of the house is therefore *Domina* (first declension). However, in Church Latin *Dominus* is exclusively reserved for The Lord in capital letters, i.e. God.

ob.

ob. for *obiit* is really short for *mortem obiit*, literally 'met death' from the verb *obeo, obire*, 'go to meet' and the accusative case of *mors, mortis*, 'death' – the corresponding adjective of which is *mortalis*, whence English 'mortal' etc.

H.I.S.

iacet in the phrase *hic iacet sepultus*, from the verb *iaceo, iacere*, 'lie' (as in lie down, not tell a lie), is often seen spelt with a j instead of an i – Medieval Latin made a distinction that didn't exist in Classical Latin between consonantal-i and i as a vowel. The j of our modern alphabet is simply an i with a tail added (see Chapter 2). The word *sepultus* is the perfect passive participle of the verb *sepelio, sepelire*, 'bury'.

R.I.P.

R.I.P. handily means 'Rest in Peace' in both English and Latin
– though the Latin verb *requiesco, requiescere*, 'rest', is in the
subjunctive mood thus more clearly expressing the sentiment as
a wish: '*May* he/she rest in peace'.

2. Academic abbreviations

As we noted in Chapter 1, Latin was the *lingua franca* of professionals
and academics throughout Europe during the Middle Ages and
even as late as the nineteenth century. In academia there arose a
proliferation of Latin acronyms for the multitude of university
qualifications, most of which remain in use today. For example:

B.A.	*Baccalaureus Artium*	Bachelor of Arts
B.D.	*Baccalaureus Divinitatis*	Bachelor of Divinity
B.L.	*Baccalaureus Legum*	Bachelor of Laws
B.Lit.	*Baccalaureus Litterarum*	Bachelor of Literature (Letters)
B.M.	*Baccalaureus Medicinae*	Bachelor of Medicine
B.Mus.	*Baccalaureus Musicae*	Bachelor of Music
B.Sc.	*Baccalaureus Scientiae*	Bachelor of Science
D.D.	*Divinitatis Doctor*	Doctor of Divinity
D.Lit.	*Doctor Litterarum*	Doctor of Literature
LL.D.	*Legum Doctor*	Doctor of Laws
M.A.	*Magister Artium*	Master of Arts
M.D.	*Medicinae Doctor*	Doctor of Medicine
Ph.D.	*Philosophiae Doctor*	Doctor of Philosophy

D.D./D.Lit./LL.D/Ph.D.

Doctor comes from the perfect passive participle, *doctus*, of the verb
doceo, docere, 'teach'. *Doctus* means 'learned, clever' and the addition
of the suffix *-tor* makes a *doctor* a 'learned man'. Nowadays we
generally restrict the use of the word to the medical profession
(though for Romans, a doctor was a *medicus*), but its original use
is preserved in the academic qualifications listed above.

Strictly speaking, the feminine version of *doctor* should add the suffix *-trix* to make a *doctrix*, but presumably the old sexist assumption was that there weren't enough learned women about to bother using a different word, so *doctor* had and still has to do for all – even though for a Roman, a 'female doctor' would have been a grammatical if not an actual oxymoron.

It's worth noting in passing that something similar seems to be happening to the English distinction between 'actor' (masculine, from *ago, agere, actus,* 'do, act') and 'actress' (feminine, via French, presumably adopted because *actrix* sounds just too clumsy?) – many actresses now routinely call themselves actors, and the old gender distinction is being phased out. English does preserve one or two *-trix* endings, such as *dominatrix*, which doesn't seem to be a Classical Latin word at all (though there is *domitrix*, which means 'she who tames'), but may have come into use because it expresses far more than just the feminine form of the masculine *dominator*.

B.A./B.Sc.

The origin of *Baccalaureus* (whence English 'Baccalaureate') remains obscure. The best guess seems to be that it is related to the Medieval Latin *Baccalaris*, a young man seeking to become a knight, though originally this was a vulgar Latin word for a farmhand. The same word gives us 'Bachelor', which only begins to be used of unmarried men in the fourteenth century (this is the sense in which it is found in Chaucer). The *bacca laureus* is the berry of a laurel, and the laurel crown was Apollo's prize for poets (hence Poet Laureate – the poet crowned with laurel), and anyone else victorious in competition either civil or military. So *Baccalaureus* denotes a prize-winning Bachelor, but not the unmarried sort.

3. *Literary abbreviations*

From Roman times, throughout the Middle Ages and into the modern era, Latin was the language of scribes and all who had anything to do with manuscripts, either writing or editing them. Which is why many editorial terms still in use today are in Latin. Here are just a selection, some very common while others are more often found in the footnotes and citations of academic works:

c.	*circa*	approximately
cf.	*confer*	compare
e.g.	*exempli gratia*	for instance (literally: for the sake of an example)
et al.	*et alii/et aliae/et alia*	and others
et seq.	*et sequens*	and the following [pages]
et seqq.	*et sequentia*	and those that follow
etc.	*et cetera*	and the rest
i.e.	*id est*	that is
i.q.	*idem quod*	the same as
ibid.	*ibidem*	in the same place
loc. cit.	*loco citato*	in the place cited
n.b.	*nota bene*	note well
ob.	*obiter*	in passing
op. cit.	*opere citato*	in the work [already] cited
p.s.	*post scriptum*	written later
q.v.	*quod vide*	see that [elsewhere]
sc.	*scilicet*	that is to say
ut sup.	*ut supra*	as above
v.	*verso*	reverse
v.	*vide*	see
v.l.	*varia lecto*	variant reading
viz.	*videlicet*	namely

loc. cit./op. cit.

Note how the ablative case expresses *place where* without needing a preposition in the phrases *loco citato* and *opere citato*. The word *citato* is actually the ablative case of the perfect participle passive *citatus* of the verb *cito, citare*, 'cite'. Literally the participle translates clumsily as 'having-been-cited'; hence the phrases mean 'in the place/work cited'.

e.g.

The ablative singular *gratia* takes the genitive case, meaning 'for the sake (of) ...' in *exempli gratia*, whereas the same word in the accusative plural with the verb *ago, agere* means to express thanks, i.e. *gratias ago tibi*, 'I give thanks to you'.

n.b./q.v.

The *nota* of *nota bene* is an example of the imperative – 'note!' – from the first conjugation verb *noto, notare*, whereas the *vide* – 'see!' – in *quod vide* is the imperative of the second conjugation verb *video, videre*. Both are simply the verb stem, but second conjugation verb stems end in -*e*, first conjugation verbs end in -*a*.

etc.

Speaking of endings in -*a*, *et cetera* literally means 'and the other things' – specifically 'things' because *cetera* is neuter plural. The second declension neuter plural ending in -*a* must be carefully distinguished from the first declension nominative and ablative singular, also ending in -*a*, otherwise confusion will result! That's just one reason why it's vital to learn not just the noun or adjective, but which declension it belongs to. The best way to do this is to learn both the nominative singular *and* the genitive singular, since the latter gives you both the stem on which the endings are added and the declension, e.g. *femina, feminae* (woman) has the stem *femin-* and is first declension (-*ae* genitive ending), whereas *vir, viri* (man) has stem *vir-* and is second declension (-*i* genitive ending).

4. *Miscellaneous*

Coins retain abbreviations because they are just too small for full-length sentences. We still tell the time using *A.M.* and *P.M.* When applying for jobs we send in our *C.V.* in the hope of earning a good salary *p.a.* And when we've proved something to our own satisfaction we say *Q.E.D.*

| A.M. | *ante meridiem* | Before midday |
| ad. lib. | *ad libitum* | As one pleases, freely |

C.V.	*Curriculum Vitae*	Summary (literally: 'race' or 'course') of life
D.G.	*Dei Gratia*	By the Grace of God
E.R.	*Elizabeth Regina*	Queen Elizabeth
F.D.	*Fidei Defensor*	Defender of the faith
infra dig.	*infra dignitatem*	Beneath one's dignity
p.a.	*per annum*	Yearly
P.M.	*post meridiem*	After midday
Q.E.D.	*quod erat demonstrandum*	That which was to be demonstrated [has been]
S.P.Q.R.	*Senatus Populusque Romanus*	The Senate and People of Rome

C.V.

Americans call it a Resumé, but a C.V. is an abbreviation familiar to all job-hunters in the U.K. and British Commonwealth countries. Like most popular Latin phrases, this one is not Roman at all, but first appeared

> ### Elizabeth II D.G. Reg. F.D
>
> Look at any British coin and you'll see this curious formula, which is short for *Elizabeth II Dei Gratia Regina Fidei Defensor* – 'Elizabeth II by the grace of God Queen Defender of the Faith'. The wording changes to *Rex* for king.

in the seventeenth century. A *curriculum* is a running race or racetrack in Classical Latin, but also a 'course' and is used here in the figurative sense of the course of a person's life, not an actual racecourse. *Vitae* is the genitive singular of *vita*, 'life' (English 'vital'), hence the phrase means 'course of life', which is to say a summary of one's professional, academic and personal experience – specifically that relevant to the job vacancy being sought. *Curriculum* is neuter singular, so the plural would be *curricula vitae* – 'the courses of one's life'.

A.M./P.M.

Note again how the prepositions in the table above work: *ante, ad, per* and *post* all taking a noun in the accusative case. *Meridies*, 'noon', gives us the adjective *meridianus*, whence the 'Greenwich meridian'.

Q.E.D.

Quod is the neuter pronoun, 'that thing'. *Demonstrandum* is the form of the verb *demonstro, demonstrare* ('demonstrate') which functions as an adjective agreeing with *quod* – this adjectival form of the verb is known as a gerundive and is passive in meaning ('to be -ed'). The gerundive with a tense of *sum, esse* (in this case, the imperfect tense) indicates obligation, i.e. 'that which must be demonstrated'. Implicit in the phrase is that the thing to be demonstrated now has been, hence it is used at the end of mathematical proofs.

Recommended reading:

J. Morwood (ed.) *A Dictionary of Latin Words and Phrases*
Oxford University Press

CHAPTER 5

ROMAN NAMES, NUMERALS, DATES & DAYS

We have inherited many things from the Romans, including their months of the year. And we still use Roman numerals, though these days only for special occasions when an 'Arabic' numeral just doesn't seem dignified enough. Fortunately, however, the old Roman system of reckoning dates has fallen into disuse, as has the Romans' method of assigning names to each other – both now seem horrendously overcomplicated. But in this chapter we'll explore all these aspects of Roman society, because all are (a) useful when it comes to reading real Latin inscriptions (for more of which see Chapters 14 and 15) and (b) inherently interesting in themselves.

ROMAN NAMES

1. *Men*

In the Republican and early Imperial period, a Roman (male) citizen typically had three names: a *praenomen*, a *nomen* and a *cognomen*. The Latin word *nomen* (genitive *nominis*) is the source of such English words as 'nominate', 'nominal' and 'nomenclature'. *Prae-* here means 'in front of, before' and *cog-* has the sense of 'added to', 'in addition to' – so a *praenomen* is the first (what we would call Christian) name, the *cognomen* the surname.

There were only a limited number of *praenomina* (forenames) in regular use, such as:

Aulus	Manius
Appius	Marcus
Caius/Gaius	Numerius
Cnaeus/Gnaeus	Publius
Decimus	Quintus
Kaeso	Servius
Lucius	Sextus

Spurius	Titus
Tiberius	Vibius

The *nomen* was the clan (*gens*) name, just as with Scottish clans today. Examples include:

Aelius	Horatius
Aurelius	Julius
Caecina	Licinius
Cornelius	Maecenas
Flavius	Tullius

The *cognomen* (surname) denoted the particular branch of the clan to which the individual belonged: they might share both *praenomen* and *nomen* with other members of the same clan. Many *cognomina* were originally nicknames that became accepted and handed down through the generations. Otherwise they might be derived from the maternal line (e.g. the Emperor Domitian derives from his mother's name, Domitilla). Examples of famous *cognomina* include:

Caesar	Crassus
Cicero ('chickpea')	Naso ('nose')
Scipio ('stick')	Vespasian

The father's *praenomen* was usually passed to the eldest son and later (from the mid-first century A.D.) to all sons.

Some famous *praenomen-nomen-cognomen* combinations:

Gaius Julius Caesar	Publius Ovidius Naso (Ovid)
Marcus Tullius Cicero	Lucius Annaeus Seneca
Marcus Licinius Crassus	Publius Vergilius Maro (Virgil)
Quintus Horatius Flaccus (Horace)	

So the man whom we know as Julius Caesar was a member of the Julii clan belonging to a particular branch whose paternal designation was Caesar. Only intimate family members would have called him Gaius. Caesar was known by his *cognomen*, presumably because there were many Julii and it would have caused confusion to use that *nomen*. But in the case of an Horatius (Horace) or a Vergilius (Virgil) or an Ovidius (Ovid), the *nomen* was sufficient. There seems to be no hard and fast rule as to which was chosen.

2. *Women*

Women were not given a distinct *praenomen*, but took the feminine form of their father's *nomen*. So, Cicero's daughter was called Tullia (from Tullius), Caesar's daughter was Julia (from Julius). If there were two daughters, the elder would be called, e.g. Julia Maior and the younger Julia Minor. If there were three or more daughters, they would be numbered Julia Prima, Julia Secunda, Julia Tertia and so on. Most women also had a *cognomen*, sometimes the feminine form of their father's, e.g. the daughter of Caecilius Metellus was called Caecilia Metella. Upon marriage a woman added her husband's name (in the genitive case, indicating possession) to her family name. So when Caecilia married Crassus she became Caecilia Metella Crassi.

3. *Slaves*

Slaves usually had just a single name, given to them by their master or the slave-dealer. A famous slave, later freed by Augustus, was Phaedrus, who translated Aesop's (Greek) fables into Latin and added many of his own. Often slave names were patronising, just like those given to black slaves on the cotton plantations of the American South centuries later, e.g. Verecundus: 'modest', Novicius: 'new boy'. If and when a slave was manumitted (freed), they usually took their master's *praenomen* and *nomen* in addition. So the slave Verecundus belonging to M. Favonius upon becoming free became Marcus Favonius Verecundus. In inscriptions this would be indicated by *M L* standing for *Marci Libertus*, 'freedman of Marcus'. The same applied to female slaves, such as Pomponia Platura, whose epitaph (see Chapter 14) reads: *Ossa Pomponiae C[aii] L[ibertae] Platurae*, 'The bones of Pomponia Platura, freedwoman of Caius.'

4. *Emperors*

Emperors used a formal series of titles, typically beginning with *Imperator* and followed by *Caesar*, then their own names, e.g. *M*.

Aurelius Antoninus, then *Augustus*. In inscriptions their relationship to illustrious predecessors is indicated, as are their military victories if any (see Chapter 14). Augustus himself, the first emperor, was *Imperator Caesar Divi Filius Augustus*, 'Emperor Caesar, Son of the Divine (man), Augustus'. The *divus* in question was Julius Caesar, at that time the only emperor to have received deification.

ROMAN NUMERALS

I	1	XLI	41
II	2	L	50
III	3	C	100
IV	4	CI	101
V	5	CC	200
VI	6	CD	400
VII	7	D	500
VIII	8	DCCC	800
IX	9	CCM	800
X	10	CM	900
XX	20	M	1000
XXI	21	MCM	1900
XXX	30	MMI	2001
XL	40	MMVI	2006

- A smaller numeral placed after a larger adds to it: XI = 11, CI = 101
- A smaller numeral placed in front of a larger subtracts: IX = 9, XC = 90
- Repeated numerals double, triple etc: XXX = 30, CC = 200
- A line drawn over a numeral multiplies it by 1000
- Actual ancient Roman usage was simpler – they just wrote IIII for 4 and VIIII for 9 and so on
- ∞ was the original Roman symbol for 1000. The D for 500 is this symbol chopped in half!
- Cardinal numbers (*unus* 'one', *duo* 'two', *tres* 'three' etc.) and Ordinal numbers (*primus* 'first', *secundus* 'second', *tertius* 'third' etc.) are adjectives and decline in exactly the same way as other adjectives. Note that only *unus, -a, -um* has a singular declension, all the others are in the plural only.

Given the unwieldy nature of these numerals it's a wonder that Roman engineers managed to build such impressive aqueducts, bridges and buildings!

Question: What number is missing?

ROMAN DATES

1. *Years*

Romans reckoned years from the traditional founding of the city of Rome, A.U.C. (*anno urbis conditae*, 'in the year of the founding of the city'), held to be what we would call the year 753 B.C. In practice, however, years were given by naming the two consuls of that year (in the ablative case), e.g. *M. Messalla et M. Pupio consulibus* (61 B.C.). This is how Classical writers such as Caesar or Livy always reckon dates.

A.U.C to A.D. and vice versa

To work out a date B.C., subtract it from 754, e.g. 700 A.U.C. (754 − 700) = 54 B.C.

To work out a date A.D., subtract 753, e.g. 769 A.U.C. (769 − 753) = A.D. 16

To convert dates B.C. into A.U.C. subtract from 754, e.g. 70 B.C. = 684 A.U.C.

To convert dates A.D. into A.U.C. add 753, e.g. A.D. 10 is 763 A.U.C.

The drawback is obvious: in order to know what year someone was talking about either you had to know by heart the entire list of consuls, or have access to that list in, say, the Roman forum.

Both these methods (A.U.C. and consulships) were abandoned during the reign of the Emperor Constantine in the early fourth century A.D., when years came to be reckoned from the (supposed) birth of Christ (*Anno Domini*), the system we still use today.

2. *Months*

Our 12 months of the year are derived from the Romans. Originally the Roman calendar only had 10 months, because, as with many primitive agricultural societies, there was no need to reckon winter days since there was no planting or harvesting to be done. So the winter 'months' were simply left blank. January and February were added later. This is why September is called the 'Seventh' month when in fact it's the ninth.

As the English word suggests, months originally marked the cycles of the moon – a very important calendar for an agricultural society. The Latin word for month is *mensis*, plural *menses*, monthly is *menstruus*, hence 'menstruation'.

The 12-month Roman calendar originally had 355 days, with an extra month being added between February and March to bring it back into line with the actual solar year. In 46 B.C. Julius Caesar hired a Greek scholar named Sosigenes to reform this old system. The new Julian calendar had 365.25 days, which in practice meant adding an extra day to February every fourth year. The new year now began on January 1st (the day on which the consuls took up their annual office), not March 1st as before.

This Julian calendar was used throughout Europe for thousands of years (it was not amended in Russia until 1918). However, there still remained a small discrepancy between the solar and calendar year of roughly seven days every 1000 years. So in the sixteenth century (when the discrepancy was up to about ten days) the Gregorian calendar (named after Pope Gregory XIII) tweaked the Julian system to omit leap years once every 100 years, except in centuries divisible by 400: 1600, 2000 etc. This new calendar was not adopted in Britain until 1752, when 11 days had to be dropped in order to bring Britain into line with the rest of Europe.

Ianuarius

From Ianus, the god who faces both backwards and forwards, thus toward the old and new years simultaneously. Ianus was for the same reason the god of doorways. The gates of his temple were only closed during times of peace (hence, rarely). English: *January, Janitor.*

Februarius

Either from the Sabine god Februus, or from *febris* ('fever'). The Romans held festivals of purification this month, most famously the Lupercalia on the 15th. English: *February, febrile* (from *febris*).

Martius

From the god Mars, originally a native Italian agricultural god only later associated with the Greek god of war, Ares. Hence this month was the time to begin planting. English: *March, Martial.*

Aprilis

Possibly derived from old Etruscan versions either of the Greek goddess Aphrodite or Apollo (Aplu). English: *April.*

Maius

From Maia, native Italian goddess, daughter of Fauna and Vulcan. English: *May.*

Iunius

From Iuno, another native Roman goddess later identified with the Greek Hera, wife of Zeus (Jupiter in Latin). Iuno was originally the goddess of female fertility. English: *June.*

Iulius

Named in honour of the deified Julius Caesar following his death in 44 B.C. Previously this month had been called simply Quintilis or Quinctilis ('fifth'). English: *July.*

Augustus

Like the preceding, named for the deified Augustus, adopted heir of Julius Caesar and first Roman Emperor. Previously called Sextilis ('sixth'). English: *August, august* (as in 'an august personage').

September, October, November, December

The seventh (7 = *septem*), eighth (8 = *octo*), ninth (9 = *novem*) and tenth (10 = *decem*) months respectively, before January and February were added (see above).

3. *The week*

The seven-day week as we know it didn't exist in Classical Roman times. However, market days (*nundinae*) occurred every ninth day (reckoned inclusively, we would say eight days).

Our modern seven-day week derives from the Jewish calendar with its regular Sabbath (Saturday). This week was only introduced during the reign of Constantine, the first Christian emperor, in the early fourth century. Note, seven in Latin is *septem*, seventh is *septimus*, whence Italian *settimana*, French *semaine* and Spanish *semana*, all meaning 'week'.

4. Days of the month

The Romans didn't have proper names for each day as we do. Instead, they reckoned days from three key points in each month: the Kalends, the Nones and the Ides, originally connected with the phases of the moon.

Kalends

The first day of the month, probably derived from the verb *calare* ('to announce, call out'). The Kalends was the day on which interest on loans were due, these were recorded in an account book or ledger called a *kalendarium*, hence English 'calendar'.

Nones

Either the fifth or the seventh day, so called as it was nine days (counting inclusively) before the Ides.

Ides

Either the thirteenth (Nones on the fifth) or the fifteenth (Nones on the seventh) day, marking the middle of the month.

The day following the Kalends, Nones and Ides were *nefasti* (ill-omened) so it was forbidden to transact any business on those days. Business days were *fasti*, days on which there was no official feast (a *festum*), also called *dies vacantes* ('empty days', English 'vacation').

The Nones fell on the fifth day, the Ides on the thirteenth, except:

> In March, July, October, May
> The Nones fall on the seventh day
> And the Ides on the fifteenth

HOW TO RECKON ROMAN DAYS

Days inbetween are counted backwards from the Kalends, Nones or Ides (*Idus*). The day immediately preceding these is *pridie* ('the day before'), while others are numbered. Note that Romans reckoned numbers *inclusively*, counting both the days inbetween and the days at either end (we would only include the day at the end). The common abbreviation for each date is given in parentheses – this is how they are often seen in inscriptions.

All the months are adjectives, agreeing with the noun *mensis* (feminine, third declension) understood.

So, for example:

Idibus Ianuaris (Id. Ian.)[1]   January 13th

ante diem octavum Idus Ianuarias (a.d. VIII Id. Ian.)[2]
                                                   January 6th

Nonis Ianuaris (Non. Ian.)[1]   January 5th

pridie Nonas Ianuarias (prid. Non. Ian.)[2]   January 4th

ante diem tertium Nonas Ianuarias (a.d. III Non. Jan.)
                                                   January 3rd

ante diem quartum Nonas Ianuarias (a.d. IV Non. Jan.)
                                                   January 2nd

Kalendis Ianuaris (Kal. Ian.)[1]   January 1st

pridie Kalendas Ianuarias (prid. Kal. Ian.)   December 31st

ante diem tertium Kalendas Ianuarias (a.d. III Kal. Ian.)
                                                   December 30th

Notes:
1   If a date falls on the Kalends, Nones or Ides, it is given in the ablative plural

2   *pridie* and *ante* are both followed by the accusative. The ordinal
number (*primus, secundus* etc.) is accusative singular, agreeing with
diem. Then accusative plural of *kalendae, nonae, idus* (all feminine)
+ accusative plural of the month as an adjective

5. *The ablative of time*

In practice, however, the system described above is by no means
the only one to be seen on ancient Roman inscriptions, let alone
in medieval or more modern sources such as dates on epitaphs in
churches or cathedrals. For the Romans, years were reckoned by the
names of of the two annually elected consuls, e.g. *Caesare et Bibulo
consulibus*, '[in the year] with Caesar and Bibulus as consuls'.

Commonly, the time in which something happens, e.g. the day of
someone's death on an epitaph, is reported in the 'plain' ablative case,
that is without the preposition *in* meaning 'on'. So, for example:

A. Excerpts from an Augustan inscription[1]

XVIII[2] K. Febr. eo die[3] Caesar Augustus appellatus est[4] ...

Prid. Non. Mart. eo die Caesar Pontifex maximus creatus est ...

IIII[5] Id. Iul. Natalis[6] divi Iuli[7]

B. Excerpts from two Epitaphs in St Albans Cathedral

Decessit octavo die Martii A.D. MDCCXXXI
Obijt Decimo Nono die[8] Januarij[9] A.D. MDCCXXXIII Aetatis
Suae[10] LIX

Notes:

1   This inscription from Cumae on the Bay of Naples gives dates
throughout the year connected with the cult of the Emperor
Augustus
2   XVIII – without ante diem or a.d.
3   eo die – ablative of time when: 'on that day'
4   appellatus est ... creatus est – perfect passives of *appello, appellare*,
'he was named', and *creo, creare*, 'he was elected'

5   IIII – note four vertical strokes, not IV
6   natalis – 'birthday'
7   divi Iuli – genitive of divus Iulius, 'of the deified Julius'
8   octavo die … decimo nono die – ablatives of time: 'on the eighth
    day' and 'on the nineteenth day'
9   Martii … Januarij – both genitive
10 etatis suae – genitive, 'of his/her age', i.e. 'aged'

CHAPTER 6

LATIN FOR GARDENERS

A. LINNAEUS AND THE *SPECIES PLANTARUM*

As we mentioned in Chapter 1, Carl Linnaeus used Latin for his system of biological classification (known as taxonomy). In 1753 he published his botanical *magnum opus*, the *Species Plantarum*, a systematic attempt to classify, as the title says, the appearance of plants. Linnaeus adopted a binomial ('two-name') system of plant nomenclature.

Linnaeus (1707-1778)

Swedish scientist Carl von Linné studied medicine but specialised in botany. In 1735 he published the first edition of his *Systema Naturae* in which he first set forth the binomial system of plant and animal names. Since scientists in all countries routinely wrote and corresponded in Latin, his book was widely and enthusiastically received. He was knighted in 1761.

Before Linnaeus there was no single, universally acknowledged method of naming plants. Ever since, Linnaeus' system has been used, with some modifications. The great advantage of his Latin naming method is that it avoids all confusion caused by the plethora of different colloquial names used in different regions of a country, not to mention the names of plants in different languages around the world.

The binomial system defines the *genus* (literally 'stock' or 'family') and the *species* (literally 'appearance' or 'shape'). These two words can also be augmented by a word or phrase to describe the specific variety or cultivar. In the convention adopted by botanists the world over, the *genus* is given first with a capital letter, followed by the *species* in lower case, both in italics, e.g.

Calendula officinalis   English Marigold

1. *Genus*

The *genus* is the primary name, often of ancient origin (the Romans called the Oak *Quercus* and the Ivy *Hedera*). Handily, some of these old Latin words are still the common plant name. Some easily identifiable Latin *genus* names are:

Chrysanthemum	*Lotus*
Clematis	*Petunia*
Dahlia	*Polyanthus*
Fuchsia	*Rosa*
Hyacinthus	*Rhododendron*
Lobelia	*Tulipa*

Familiar names like these are often given as a simple abbreviation, such as *C. alpina* (Alpine Clematis). It's also easy to guess that *Nicotiana* is the Tobacco plant, *Lilium* is a Lily and *Tulipa* is a Tulip. Less easy, unless you already know, that *Impatiens* is the Busy Lizzie and *Acer* is a Maple tree.

2. *Species*

The *species* name provides an adjectival description to accompany the *genus*. The Opium Poppy, for example, has the expressive tag *Papaver somniferum*, 'sleep-bringing'. A plant described as *praecox* means it flowers early ('premature'), an *annuus* flowers annually, while *sempervirens* ('always blooming') or *semperflorens* ('always flowering') is a perennial.

Commonly used of rose bushes, *floribunda* is a neo-Latin coinage to describe plants that produce large groups of flowers. And if you see a plant species described as *officinalis*, it's a good bet that it's of either medicinal or culinary use, since the word derives from Latin *officina*, a workshop or manufactory –

> **Cultivars**
>
> A cultivar is a variety produced by selective breeding rather than nature. A cultivar name is not always Latinised and is printed in standard type in inverted commas e.g. *Elaeagnus pungens* 'Maculata' (Thorny Eleagnus) or *Geranium cinereum* 'Ballerina'.

indicating that the plant is of practical value, e.g. *Rosmarinus officinalis* (Rosemary).

Other *species* names are purely physically descriptive, such as *splendens* ('shining'), *repens* ('creeping') and *pendens* ('hanging') – all incidentally Latin present participles. Colours used adjectivally in agreement with the *genus* noun are also a common identifier, e.g. *albus, -a, -um* ('white'), *purpureus, -a, -um* ('purple') or *luteus, -a, -um* ('yellow').

Species names such as *wilsonii, douglasii* or *davidii* commemorate the names of those who first discovered the plants. (If the abbreviation *L.* is used, the discoverer was our man Linnaeus himself.) Other descriptions such as *lusitanica* (Portugal), *patagonica* (Patagonia) or *japonica* (Japan) tell us the plant's geographical origins. The *species* can also be subdivided into subspecies (sometimes with the abbreviation *subsp.* or *ssp.*), e.g. *Euphorbia characias subsp. wulfenii*.

3. *Varieties and hybrids*

Naturally occurring varieties – the result of differing ecological conditions in different parts of the world – are indicated by *var.*, e.g. *Geranium sanguinium var. striatum*, though as with subspecies the abbreviation is not always included.

When two *species* are interbred to produce a hybrid, the cross is marked, appropriately enough, by a cross or multiplication sign, e.g. *Cystius x praecox* 'Warminster' (Warminster Broom). Sometimes, plants end up with two 'official' names, usually because a plant has been reclassified, but the older name remains in use. In this case the other name or synonym (*syn.*), is sometimes mentioned, e.g. *Aurinia saxatilis syn. Alyssum saxatile*.

4. *Roses*

The case with roses is slightly different. Numerous cultivated forms have been derived from the eglantine (*Rosa rubiginosa*) and dogrose (*Rosa canina*) native to Europe and Asia. The *species* name, though, is usually omitted, since it is the specific cultivar that is of interest. But often the cultivar name only applies to a particular country, because roses tend to be named after local people or places that don't necessarily have meaning elsewhere (e.g. *Rosa* 'Betty Boop',

Rosa 'Queen Mother', *Rosa* 'Anna Ford', *Rosa* 'Hampshire' and many more). In 1979, a new international standard was adopted for rose cultivar names, in which the first three letters represent the name of the breeder, so for example the cultivar known in the U.K. as *Rosa* 'Gertrude Jekyll' is internationally known as *Rosa* 'Ausbord', the 'Aus' part from its breeder David Austin.

Of Pets & Men

What applies to plants also applies to animals. The domestic cat, for example, belongs to the genus *Felis*, species *cattus* of the family *Felidae* (large cats such as lions and tigers belong to the genus *Panthera*). The domestic dog belongs to the same genus and species as the wolf, *Canis lupus*. But the family dog is a subspecies, *Canis lupus familiaris* – 'household wolf'!

Two third declension nouns:

feles, felis (f)	cat, hence 'feline'
canis, canis (m/f)	dog, hence 'canine'

Linnaeus designated humans as *Homo sapiens*, 'wise man'. *Homo* means 'man' in the sense of all human beings not man in the narrow gender sense (in Latin, a specific man is a *vir*). *Sapiens* is the present participle of the verb *sapio, sapere* – 'taste' or 'smell' when applied to the senses, but also 'discern' in the mental realm, that is the ability to make rational judgements. So *sapiens* means 'judicious', 'sensible', 'wise' – qualities that we humans don't demonstrate often enough.

B. GARDENING PREFIXES & SUFFIXES

As we've discovered, plant names are usually descriptive – so *Magnolia stellata* is the Star Magnolia, while *Rhododendron luteum* has yellow flowers. With the help of a Latin dictionary you should be able to identify many other Latin (or Latinate) nouns or adjectives used to describe plants. But it's also helpful to know some of the Latin prefixes and suffixes that are commonly appended to plant names. Here are just a few examples:

a-/an-
without, lacking, e.g. *apetalus* 'without petals'

acri-

acrid, sharp, e.g. *acrifolia*, 'sharp-leaved'

alb-

white, e.g. *albiflorens*, 'white-flowering'

arg-

silver, e.g. *argophyllus*, 'silver-leaved'

aurant-

orange, e.g. *aurantifolia*, 'orange-leaved'

aure-

golden, e.g. *aurespina*, 'golden-spined'

brevi-

short, e.g. *brevicaulis*, 'short-stemmed'

chlor-

green, e.g. *chloranthus*, 'green-flowered'

chrys-

golden yellow, e.g. *Chrysanthemum*, 'golden flower'

-fer-

bearing, producing, e.g. *fructifera*, 'fruit-bearing'

foli- or -foli-

leaves, e.g. *latifolia*, 'flat-leaved'

flor-

a flower, e.g. *floribunda*, 'abundantly-flowering'

herb-

not woody, i.e. herbaceous

leuc-

white, e.g. *Leucadendron*, 'silver tree'

mela-
> black, e.g. *Melaleuca*, 'black and white'

ochr-
> yellow, e.g. *Ochrocarpus*, 'yellow fruit'

palle-/palli-
> pale, e.g. *pallidiflora*, 'pale flower'

rhod-
> rose red, e.g. *Rhododendron*, 'rose tree'

virid-
> green, e.g. *viridiflora*, 'green-flowers'

xanth-
> yellow, e.g. *xanthocarpus*, 'yellow-fruited'

C. A GARDENERS' GLOSSARY

The Latin origins of some key botanical words:

bulb
> Latin *bulbus*, 'bulb', 'onion', from Greek βολβος, a hyacinth

flower
> Latin *flos, floris*. Both in Latin and English, 'flower' figuratively denotes the best, the finest, hence English 'flourish'. The flour that is used to make bread originally derives from this meaning, i.e. the best part of the wheat. 'Foliage' is also a related word.

fork
> Latin *furca*, 'a pitch-fork' but also an instrument of punishment placed over the neck of slaves to which their arms were tied.

horticulture
> A compound word derived from Latin *hortus*, 'a garden', and the participle *cultus* of the verb *colo, colere*, 'to cultivate'. It is first recorded by the Oxford English Dictionary in 1678.

petal

Latin *petalum*, a non-Classical word after the Greek πεταλον, 'leaf'

plant

Latin *planta*, 'a green twig', 'a cutting', though it can also mean the 'sole of the foot'.

trowel

Latin *trulla*, 'a stirring-spoon', diminutive of *trua*, 'ladle'. The name was applied to a medieval tool used by masons for applying cement, which was then adapted for use in the garden.

trunk

Latin *truncus*, 'the stem of a tree'. Also used in both Latin and English for the main part of the human body. (Cicero uses the word pejoratively to mean 'blockhead!')

Recommended reading:

W. Neal   *Gardener's Latin: A Lexicon*
Algonquin Books
A comprehensive dictionary of Latin plant names and their meanings.

R. Bird   *Gardener's Latin*
Hearst Books
An illustrated guide book, divided into chapters that focus on flower and leaf colours, fragrance, habitat, size etc.

W.T. Stearn   *Botanical Latin*
Timber Press
First published in 1966, this is the bible for serious botanists.

CHAPTER 7

MOTTOES

Latin is peculiarly well suited to motto-making: its conciseness, its lack of both definite and indefinite articles, and its inflected forms all mean that Latin has the ability to express in just a few words what would take many more in a modern language. From about the fifteenth century onwards, heraldic crests began to be adorned with suitably pithy Latin mottoes, each a brief *sententia* intended to express the family's pretensions or aspirations. Countries, cities, organisations and institutions have also adopted Latin mottoes for much the same reasons: even the most prosaic 'mission statement' seems profound when expressed in that venerable and ancient language. Below you will find just a tiny selection, but hopefully a representative one, of Latin mottoes old and new:

1. Family mottoes
2. Military mottoes
3. School and College mottoes
4. Football team mottoes
5. Latin mottoes in the U.S.A.
6. Other mottoes

War cries

Some mottoes originated from war-cries used in battle to rally troops to their clan, their overlord or their emperor. The British Royal Family's motto – *Dieu et mon droit* ('God and my right') – is said to be of this kind, supposedly Edward III's rallying cry during the Battle of Crécy in 1346.

1. Family mottoes

orbis non sufficit   Bond

The fictional motto of the Bond family first appeared in the 1969 film *On Her Majesty's Secret Service* (starring George Lazenby) and reappeared in English as the title of 1999's *The World is Not Enough*. It's a simple noun-verb sentence with the negative *non* before the verb – if the negative came before the noun the emphasis would be altered: 'It is *not* the world that is enough'.

non sine periculo/dum spiro, spero   Walker

The Walker clan seems to have acquired at least two mottoes – one with no verbs, the other with two but no nouns. The preposition *sine*, 'without', always takes the ablative case, so the second declension neuter noun *periculum*, 'danger' changes to *periculo*. *Spiro* and *spero* are two simple first person indicative verbs, both first conjugation, prefaced by *dum*, 'while': *spiro, spirare* gives English 'respiration' as well as 'inspiration'; *spero, sperare* didn't find its way into English but is unchanged in modern Italian, 'hope'.

non nobis, sed omnibus   Ash

Two examples of the dative case in action. *Nobis* is dative plural of the personal pronoun *ego*, 'I', plural *nos*, 'we'. *Omnibus* is dative plural of the adjective *omnis*, 'every, all' – here used substantively, that is not as an adjective but standing in for a noun. So, the motto is simply 'not for us, but for everyone'.

Omnibus

The dative plural of *omnis*, 'all', an *Omnibus* is a mode of transport 'for everyone'. The *-bus* ending characterises third, fourth and fifth declension dative and ablative plurals. *Nihil exspectore in omnibus*, announced Kenneth Williams' Caesar in *Carry On Cleo*, 'No spitting on the public transport'!

noli irritare leonem   Cooper

This motto exemplifies a useful grammatical construction. Verbs such as *volo*, 'I want', *nolo*, 'I don't want', *malo*, 'I prefer', as well as *possum*, 'I can' are typically accompanied, as here, by the infinitive of another verb (it's similar in English, 'I want/don't want *to do* it'. 'I can *do* it' = 'I am able *to do* it'). Here, *noli* is the imperative: 'don't provoke the lion'.

2. Military mottoes

semper fidelis   U.S. Marine Corps

Also the title of a famous Sousa march. *Fidelis* is usually translated as 'faithful', but perhaps 'steadfast' is better in this context: 'Always steadfast'?

per ardua ad astra   Royal Air Force

Both prepositions *per* and *ad* take the accusative case. The only accusatives ending in -*a* are neuter plurals, so both *ardua* and *astra* must be neuter plurals of (a) *arduum*, adjective, 'a difficult [thing]' and (b) *astrum*, 'a star'. So, 'through difficulties/hardships to the stars'.

sic itur ad astra   Canadian Air Force

This one uses the third person singular passive of the verb *eo, ire*, 'go'. The passive *itur* is only ever used impersonally in Latin, that is to say it does not have a subject. (Common impersonal verbs in English are those connected with the weather, e.g. 'it's raining', 'it's snowing'). A literal rendering – 'Thus it goes to the stars' – is not really possible, so English needs to substitute a noun for the Latin verb, i.e. 'That is the way to the stars'.

3. *School and College mottoes*

donorum Dei dispensatio fidelis   Harrow School

This motto is emblazoned in large, friendly letters on the main school building at the summit of Harrow-on-the-Hill in north-west London. The word-order in English is almost the exact reverse of the Latin: *fidelis*, adjective, 'faithful' (like the U.S. Marine Corps above); a *dispensatio* is an English 'dispensation', i.e. a 'weighing out', 'management'; *donorum* is genitive plural of neuter *donum*, 'gift'; whose gifts? those of *Deus* ('deity') – *Dei* is genitive singular. So, 'Faithful stewardship of the gifts of God'.

sapere aude   Manchester Grammar

Aude is the imperative singular – that's an order! – of *audeo, audere*, 'dare'. (What do you think *Qui audet, vincit* means?). *Sapio, sapere* is 'taste' or 'smell', so mentally, 'discern' or 'be wise'. The phrase is a quote from the Roman poet Horace, 'Dare to be wise'.

dat Deus incrementum   Westminster School

Incrementum is neuter accusative – English 'increment' – 'growth', 'increase'. Normal Latin word-order would put the verb *do, dare* at the end. So, 'God gives growth'.

floreat Etonia   Eton School

The subjunctive of a verb in the third person typically expresses a wish or a command, 'may it ...', 'let it ...' (note that the imperative can only be used in the second person, that is to give an order directly to someone, not indirectly). *Floreo, florere*, 'flower', 'flourish' would be *floret* in the indicative. The related noun is *flos, floris* (English 'floral' – see Latin for Gardeners, Chapter 6). 'Let Eton flourish'.

hinc lucem et pocula sacra   Cambridge University

Hinc is an indeclinable adverb, 'from here'. *Lux, lucis*, accusative *lucem*, third conjugation, is 'light' but metaphorically 'elucidation', 'enlightenment'. A *poculum* – neuter – is a drinking cup but also 'a drink' or 'a draught'. Adjective *sacra* agrees by being neuter plural accusative with *pocula*, 'sacred draughts' – presumably from the spring of knowledge? The verb needs to be supplied. The elegant but long-winded English translation is 'From the university we receive enlightenment and knowledge'.

Dominus illuminatio mea   Oxford University

A legacy of Oxford's ecclesiastical history, these are the first words of Psalm 27 in the Vulgate (see Chapter 9, Church Latin). *Dominus* in Classical Latin is 'master', as in the head of the household, but in Biblical Latin it is always 'Lord', i.e. God. *Illuminatio* – feminine, hence *mea* – is another Biblical Latin word for 'enlightening', Christ being referred to as the *Illuminator*, i.e. 'The Lord is my light'.

draco dormiens nunquam titillandus   Hogwarts

The *alma mater* of a certain boy wizard, Hogwarts has as its school motto an apt warning: *draco, draconis* (masculine) is a serpent in general, but what is specifically meant here of course is a dragon. *Dormio, dormire*, naturally, is 'sleep', *dormiens* being the present participle – literally 'while -ing' – nominative masculine in agreement with *draco*. *Nunquam* (sometimes spelt *numquam*) is 'never', 'under no circumstances'. *Titillo, titillare*, 'tickle', 'provoke' or 'stimulate sensually' (that latter gives us English 'titillate', presumably not what is meant here) is given in the gerundive, the form of a verb as a passive adjective: 'to be tickled/provoked'. *Titillandus* is masculine nominative, adjectivally agreeing with *draco*. Understand *est*, which taken with the gerundive is the Latin equivalent of 'must'. Literally: 'A sleeping dragon must never be tickled [or provoked]'; paraphrase as 'Let sleeping dragons lie'.

4. *Football team mottoes*

nil satis nisi optimum   Everton

Nil or *nihil* is 'nothing'; *satis* (English 'satisfy') is 'sufficient/ enough'; *nisi*, 'except/unless'; *optimum*, 'best' is the irregular superlative of *bonus*, 'good'. The verb *est* needs to be supplied. The equivalent English expression needs a 'but': 'Nothing but the best is good enough'.

superbia in proelia   Manchester City

A *proelium*, neuter, is a 'battle', so *proelia* must be accusative plural following the preposition *in*; *superbia* is 'pride' or 'arrogance' – presumably ablative rather than nominative singular, '[We go] with pride into battles'.

victoria concordia crescit   Arsenal

Both *victoria* and *concordia* are first declension nouns, one must be nominative (subject of the verb *crescit*) and the other ablative singular (if there were two nominatives, the verb would be plural). Natural word order suggests 'Victory increases through harmony' but 'Harmony increases through victory' works just as well. A good example of deliberate vagueness.

vincit omnia industria   Bury

A nice paraphrase of Virgil's famous tag *omnia vincit amor*, the football team of Lancashire industrial town Bury prefers to think that *industria*, 'hard work' is really what conquers 'all things' (*omnia* – neuter plural). Note the change in word-order: Virgil's line emphasises the direct object *omnia*, but by putting its subject last and the verb first, Bury's motto gives added weight to *industria*.

5. Latin mottoes in the U.S.A.

A. The Great Seal

The Latin mottoes on the Great Seal of the U.S.A. – the design begun in 1776 and finalised in 1782 – reflect the aims and ambitions of America's Founding Fathers. One side of the Seal features a pyramid whose peak is an 'all-seeing' disembodied eye; the reverse has an eagle and the Stars and Stripes.

annuit coeptis

A difficult one this, since the subject has to be supplied (some mottoes take conciseness to extremes). The third conjugation verb *adnuo* (or *annuo*), *adnuere*, 'nod at/to', 'assent to', takes the dative case in the sense of 'favourable to ...', so *coeptis* is dative plural of the second declension neuter noun *coeptum*, 'a beginning', 'an undertaking'. 'X nods at/is favourable to our beginnings'. Who is X? According to Charles Thomson, designer of the Seal, who adapted the phrase from a line of Virgil, the answer is Providence (God), symbolised by the eye over the pyramid.

novus ordo seclorum

Underneath the Roman numerals for 1776 on the Seal, this motto takes the form nominative adjective-noun in agreement followed by another noun in the genitive plural. Normal Latin word-order places the adjective after its noun, so here the adjective *novus*, 'new', is emphasised by coming first. *Ordo, ordinis* is a 'row', 'rank', hence 'order' (English 'ordinal'). The second declension neuter noun *saeculum* is 'a generation', 'a century' (q.v. French *Siécle*) or an indefinite period of time, 'an age'. *Seclorum* is a contraction of Classical Latin *saeculorum*. 'A new order of the ages'.

> **Secular**
>
> The English word 'secular' derives from Latin *saeculum*, which was often used by Christians in the sense of pertaining to generations of men – worldly as opposed to godly. *In saecula saeculorum* is a Biblical Latin expression meaning 'for ever and ever'.

e pluribus unum

The American eagle is depicted holding a scroll in its beak inscribed with this famous phrase. The preposition *e/ex* is always followed by the ablative case, so *pluribus* is ablative plural of the third declension comparative adjective *plus, pluris* (derived from *multus*), 'many', whence English 'plural'. *Unum* is accusative singular – remember that 'one' is always singular, all other numbers are only plural. 'From the many one'.

B. Some State mottoes

Five examples of State mottoes in Latin:

regnat populus Arkansas

Populus (genitive *populi*) is a collective noun, singular not plural, so the verb *regno, regnare* is third-person singular. In English, by contrast, 'people' is the plural of a singular 'person' so we would say, 'The people [they] reign', with the verb being plural.

justitia omnibus District of Columbia

Omnibus is dative plural of adjective *omnis* and usually, as here, means something 'for all'; in this case that something is *iustitia*, 'justice' (remember that the modern 'j' is a medieval invention to express the consonantal-i of Classical Latin: 'j' is just an 'i' with a little hook added to the base). Since Washington D.C. is the home of the US government as well as the Supreme Court, the phrase is an apt summation of D.C.'s founding ideal.

salus populi suprema lex esto Missouri

Esto is the singular imperative of *sum, esse*. Whereas the indicative (stating a fact) is *es*, 'you are', the imperative gives a command, '(you) be!'. However, *esto* can also be used in the third-person as a command in place of the third-person subjunctive: 'let him/her/it be': contrast with the Biblical *fiat lux*, 'let there be light!', using the subjunctive of *fio, fieri* instead of *sum*. So the motto translates as, 'Let the law [*lex*, nominative] be the highest [*suprema*, superlative adjective, also nominative] safety [*salus*, noun, also nominative] of the people [*populi*, genitive].'

Lex and *salus* are both nominative because *sum* does not take a direct object but a *complement* in the same case as the subject. The same is true of English, which means both Latin and English can happily reverse the word-order: 'Let the supreme safety of the people be the law'. The adjective *suprema* (from *superus, -a, -um*, 'higher') being feminine and also nominative could apply equally to *lex* or *salus*.

esse quam videri   North Carolina

North Carolina was the only one of the original 13 states not to have a motto – a situation only remedied in 1893. The motto chosen then neatly provides us with examples of both an active and a passive infinitive. *Esse* is, of course, 'to be'; but although *videri* is the passive infinitive of *video, videre*, 'see', it does not mean 'to be seen': rather the passive of *video* is usually translated as 'seems'. The adverb *quam* when used as a conjunction simply = 'than', so the motto becomes, 'to be (rather) than to seem'. An allusion, perhaps, to the difference between an independent state and a colony?

sic semper tyrannis   Virginia

Notoriously these were the words apparently quoted by assassin John Wilkes Booth after he shot President Lincoln in 1865. A *tyrannus* (genitive *tyranni*) is an absolute ruler, a 'tyrant'; *tyrannis* is the dative plural. The dative case typically implies that the person in the dative is either a gainer or a loser, which was tragically true for Lincoln that night. *Semper*, 'always' (as in *semper fidelis*) and *sic*, 'thus, so' compactly express the literal sentiment: 'thus always to tyrants'; a more elegant circumlocution might be, 'Such is always the fate of tyrants'.

6. *Other mottoes*

ad maiorem Dei gloriam   Jesuit order

The preposition *ad* takes the accusative case. *Gloria* is the noun, while *maior* is the irregular comparative of the adjective *magnus, -a, -um*. 'To the greater glory ...' – it's crying out for an 'of ...' and sure enough we get the genitive of *Deus* to finish the sentence.

ex luna scientia   Apollo 13 mission
Another prepositional phrase: *e*/*ex* takes the ablative case, here
of *luna* (first declension feminine). *Scientia*, 'knowledge' is a noun
derived from the verb *scio, scire*, 'know'. So a *scient*ist is someone
with knowledge. Ironically, of course, this was the one Apollo
flight that didn't make it to the moon (as chronicled in the
movie starring Tom Hanks).

citius, altius, fortius   The Olympic motto
A handy reminder that the neuter form of the comparative
adjective looks the same as the comparative adverb. So this
motto could be translated as either three comparative adverbs:

Adverb	Comparative adverb
cito	citius
alte	altius
fortiter	fortius

Cito, 'quickly'. *Alte*, 'highly'. *Fortiter*, 'strongly'. The comparative
adverb in English means 'more –ly'.

Or, three comparative adjectives, all neuter:

Adjective	Comparative adjective (neuter)
citus, -a, -um	citius
altus, -a, -um	altius
fortis, -e	fortius

Citus, 'fast'. *Altus*, 'high'. *Fortis*, 'strong'. The comparative in
English adds '-er' to the end of each adjective.

orare est laborare, laborare est orare   Benedictine order
Oro, orare is 'pray', *laboro, laborare* is 'work'. Here these two
infinitives function as nouns, so translate as 'praying is working,
working is praying' rather than 'to pray is to work ...'.

unus pro omnibus, omnes pro uno   Seahaven
Seahaven is the fictional setting of the 1998 movie *The Truman
Show*, in which Jim Carrey plays a man who is unknowingly the

star of his own soap opera surrounded by a town full of actors. A witty reference to Truman's situation, the motto is a familiar phrase disguised in Latin garb. The preposition *pro*, 'for' takes the ablative case, here both plural *omnibus* from nominative singular *omnis* – 'every', plural 'all' – and singular *uno* from nominative *unus* – 'one'.

CHAPTER 8

LATIN FOR DOCTORS & LAWYERS

From ancient times throughout the Middle Ages and up until the nineteenth century, Latin was the spoken and written language of most professions. Doctors and Lawyers especially have retained much of this Latin (a) because they require precise, unambiguous terminology and (b) because saying something in Latin sounds so much more impressive than the same expression in the vernacular.

Each profession evolved a specific vocabulary of useful terms, often in abbreviated form. Some have even made it to primetime TV when a dashing young hospital doctor says 'Get him to the O.R., *stat.*' or a detective in a courtroom drama asks, 'What's the murderer's *M.O.?*'. Here are just a small selection of each:

1. *Medical phrases & abbreviations*

admov.	*admove*
agit	*agita*

Both imperative commands of second conjugation *admoveo, admovere* – 'apply' – and first conjugation *agito, agitare* – 'shake/ stir' – (English 'agitate') respectively.

alt. h.	*alternis horis*
H.S.	*hora somni*
Q.D.	*quaque die*
Q.H.	*quaque hora*

Hora, horae is a first declension noun, so *horis* (in *alternis horis*) is ablative plural and *hora* (in *hora somni*) is ablative singular. *Somni* is genitive of second declension masculine *somnus* – 'in the hour of sleep' (i.e. at bedtime), but *alternis horis*, 'in alternate hours'. *Quaque*, 'each' is the ablative of *quisque* (feminine *quaeque*) agreeing with the feminine ablatives *hora* and *die* (from fifth declension *dies, diei*, 'day') – 'every hour/day'.

Latin in Dentistry

- *dens, dentis,* 'tooth'
- *occludo, occludere,* 'close', gives 'Occlusal', the biting surface of a tooth
- *bucca, buccae,* 'cheek', so 'Buccal', the sides of a tooth
- *gingiva, gingivae,* 'gum', so 'gingivitis'
- *caries, cariei,* 'decay'

S.I.D.	*semel in die*
B.I.D.	*bis in die*
T.I.D.	*ter in die*

'One' is *unus,* but 'once' is *semel. In* takes the ablative – the time in which something is to be done – Latin typically uses the ablative in expressions involving time: 'once/twice/three times a day'.

N.R.	*non repetatur*
Q.S.	*quantum sufficiat*

Both expressions use the subjunctive. The present passive subjunctive of the verb *repeto, repetere,* 'seek again/ask back' is here used impersonally: 'It may not be repeated' – this is how Latin gives an indirect order (verb in the third person), since the imperative can only be used to give a direct order (verb in the second person). *Sufficiat* is present subjunctive active of *sufficio, sufficere:* 'as much as may suffice'.

E.M.P.	*ex modo prescripto*

The verb *praescribo, praescribere* is formed from *scribo, scribere,* 'write' and the prefix *pre-.* It means 'set out in writing', hence 'prescribe'. The neuter participle is *praescriptum,* 'prescribed' – here in the ablative following the preposition *ex:* 'in the manner prescribed'.

stat.	*statim*
U.D.	*ut dictum*

ut with an indicative (not subjunctive) verb just means 'as' or 'how'. *Dico, dicere,* 'say' has the neuter perfect participle passive *dictum,* 'a saying', 'a command', so 'take as directed'. (An *obiter dictum* is something said 'in passing'). *Statim* is an adverb which can also mean 'steadfastly', but is used by doctors when something needs to be done right away.

N.P.O.	*nil per os*
P.O.	*per os*
P.C.	*post cibum*
A.C.	*ante cibum*
P.M.	*post mortem*

Note the prepositions *ante*, 'before', *post*, 'after' and *per*, 'through/ by' are followed by the accusative case. *Os, oris*, third declension neuter, is 'mouth', hence 'oral'; *cibus, cibi*, 'food', is second declension masculine; *mors, mortis*, 'death', is third declension feminine, whence 'mortal'.

in utero

in vitro

Two familiar little phrases that nicely illustrate the use of the preposition *in* + ablative case, meaning 'in' (whereas *in* + accusative means 'into'). *Uterus* is Latin for 'womb', masculine second declension (though it also has a neuter form *uterum*). *Vitrum*, 'glass', is neuter second declension, from which we get the English adjective 'vitreous', also commonly used in medicine.

In vitro literally means '(with)in the glass', often referring to a test-tube as in '*in vitro* fertilisation' (whence test-tube babies). But it can also mean any biological experiment conducted in a controlled laboratory environment: as opposed to *in vivo*, (from the adjective *vivus, -a, -um*, 'living'), which is an experiment done (with)in a living organism.

cura te ipsum

A medical *dictum* that urges physicians to ensure they are healthy and well before treating patients, this is actually a famous quote from the Vulgate Bible (see Chapter 9): *Medice, cura te ipsum*, 'Physician, heal thyself!' (Luke IV/23). *Medice* is the vocative case of second declension noun *medicus* (to the Romans a *doctor* was a 'learned man', an academic in modern parlance, while medicine was a far humbler profession). *Cura* is the imperative of *curo, curare*, 'take care of', 'minister to'. The accusative *te* (nominative *tu*), 'you' is reinforced by the accusative of *ipse*, 'I myself', so the literal translation is 'take care of your [own] self'.

primum non nocere

This is one of the central precepts of the medical profession: 'first do no harm'. If, for example, a certain treatment is known to have harmful effects but only uncertain benefits, this *dictum* may come into play and prevent the physician from prescribing it. Contrary to popular belief the phrase is not a part of the ancient Hippocratic oath, but has been in use since the mid-nineteenth century.

In Classical Latin, the accusative (*primum*) + the infinitive (*nocere*) construction is characteristic of indirect statements (e.g. 'He said that ...') but also with certain verbs such as *volo*, 'I wish', and *nolo*, 'I don't want'. Here we need to supply a suitable verb such as *volo*, i.e. 'I desire [that] first you do no harm'.

pro re nata

Res, rei is a fifth declension noun, feminine, 'thing, matter, business'; *nata* is the perfect participle of the deponent verb *nascor*, 'born', here meaning 'constituted', so the phrase means 'under present circumstances'.

secundum artem

Secundum is a preposition followed by the accusative of third declension feminine *ars, artis*: 'according to one's skill', i.e. use your own judgement. Confusingly, *secundum* can also function as an adverb meaning 'after'; and it is also an adjective, *secundus, -a, -um*, which means 'the second' or 'following'. Hopefully when you next encounter it the context will show which sense is meant.

2. Legal words & phrases

affidavit
alias
alibi
versus (vs.)

Affidavit is the third person singular perfect tense of *affido, affidare* (a verb you won't find in a standard Latin dictionary, since it's a late-Latin coinage), 'pledge'; so literally it means '(s)he pledged', i.e. a sworn statement. *Alias* is the adverb of the adjective *alius*, 'another', meaning 'otherwise' or 'at another time', i.e. having one name at one time, another name at another. *Alibi* is just 'elsewhere', 'at another place'.

Versus in Classical Latin is the perfect passive participle of the verb *verto, vertere*, 'turn' and it means 'turned towards, facing'; so in legalese it came to mean 'against', as the two opposing parties in court 'turn against' each other. (Classical legal Latin used the preposition *in* + the accusative to mean 'against' as in Cicero's speech *In Verrem*, 'Against Verres'.)

corpus delicti
in flagrante delicto

The verb *delinquo, delinquere* means 'to commit a crime', whence English 'delinquent'. The perfect participle passive is *delictus* – *delicti* is the genitive case, *delicto* ablative. *Corpus* refers to the 'body' of evidence, i.e. proof that a crime has occurred. *In* takes the ablative of present participle *flagrans*, from the first conjugation verb *flagro, flagrare*, 'burn', 'burn with passion', so literally 'in the blazing crime', i.e. caught red-handed.

de facto
de jure

Preposition *de*, 'according to', plus the ablative. *Factus* is the perfect participle passive of *facio, facere*, 'to do', hence 'something done', 'a deed', English 'fact'. *Ius, iuris* is 'law', usually spelt with the Medieval *j* instead of Classical Latin *i*.

habeas corpus

A legal term, *habeas corpus* dates back to the fourteenth century and was formalised in English law by the Habeas Corpus Act of 1679. A writ of *habeas corpus* issued by a judge is a commandment to bring any person into custody before the court before a specified time has elapsed. Its purpose is to prevent an individual from being unlawfully imprisoned: 'You [the accuser] must produce the body [the accused]'.

The verb *habeo, habere*, 'have', in Medieval Latin expressions (of which this is one) sometimes does the work of the Classical Latin verb *debeo, debere*, 'ought' in the sense of a moral obligation. So in this case the translation is not 'You may have the body' (*habeas* being present subjunctive) but more like 'You have a duty to produce the body'.

Corpus, 'body', is a familiar noun, from which English gets such words as 'corpse', 'corporeal' (of the body, so an *incorporeal* person is a ghost) and 'corporal' (as in corporal punishment, i.e. that which is inflicted on the body). A *corpus* is also a 'body' of work, as in 'the Shakespearian corpus'.

modus operandi (M.O.)
onus probandi

'Mode of operating' and 'burden of proof' (literally 'of proving'). Both phrases use the gerund – that is the form a Latin verb takes when it is used as a noun. *Operandi* is the gerund, in the genitive case, of the verb *operor* (alternate form *opero, operare*); *probandi* is the genitive gerund of *probo, probare* ('probate'). It's the same in English, where 'operating' is a noun derived from the verb 'to operate' and 'proving' comes from 'to prove'.

pro tempore (pro tem.)
sine die (S.D.)

Two prepositional phrases about time, with both *pro* and *sine* taking the ablative case of *tempus*, 'time' and *dies*, day', respectively – Latin typically puts time expressions in the ablative case. 'For the time being [temporarily]' and 'Without a day [indefinitely]', as in 'case adjourned *pro tem.* or *sine die*'.

nolo prosequi
nolo contendere

When *nolo* is accompanied by another verb, that verb is always in the infinitive (*prosequi* from the deponent verb *prosequor*). It's the same in English: 'I don't wish *to* prosecute', i.e. I am dropping my lawsuit; 'I don't wish *to* contend', i.e. I am not defending my case – which in legal terms is not quite the same as pleading guilty, since it allows a defendant the option of presenting a defence in any subsequent trial.

pro bono
cui bono

Preposition *pro*, 'for', takes the ablative of *bonus*. The complete phrase is *pro bono publico*, 'for the public good', that is a lawyer doing public legal aid work rather than taking the usual private fee. *Cui* is dative of the interrogative adjective *qui*? 'For whose good?', i.e. who benefits?

sub poena
sub judice

Preposition *sub*, 'under' (English 'submarine') plus the ablative. A *poena, poenae* is a 'penalty/punishment', so a *sub poena* is a summons to attend the court under threat of punishment for failing to show up. *Iudex, iudicis* is a judge – as in 'I cannot comment about the case, since it is currently *sub judice*'.

Four argumenta

Some formal arguments often cited by lawyers, but also in academic disciplines, notably Philosophy:

ad hominem

An *argumentum ad hominem* is one directed at a person's character rather than what they are saying. So a lawyer may choose to attack a witness on the grounds that they are a bad person therefore their testimony is untrustworthy. In Logic, but not necessarily in the law courts, such an argument is fallacious since it fails to address the substance of the issue but irrelevantly attacks the person uttering it.

The little preposition *ad* is always followed in Latin by a noun or adjective in the accusative case, in this instance the accusative of *homo*, 'man'.

a fortiori
a posteriori
a priori

Literally 'from the stronger', an *a fortiori* argument is one that demonstrates a particular proposition is *even more certain* than another. So, for example, from the proposition that 'All men are mortal', we can argue *a fortiori* that it is *even more certain* that 'All Englishmen are mortal'.

A posteriori and *a priori* literally mean 'from the latter' and 'from the former' respectively. In Law, an *a priori* argument is one based on hypothesis alone rather than any particular facts of the case. In Philosophy it is a deductive argument from reasoning alone, not empirical facts or observation. *A posteriori* is the reverse of *a priori*, that is an argument based on the observed facts of the case (in Law) or on empirical knowledge (in Philosophy, *inductive* rather than *deductive*). So in Logic, the proposition 'All unmarried men are bachelors' is *a priori*, since it is necessarily true that 'bachelor' means 'unmarried man'. More contentiously, philosopher René Descartes believed that the proposition *Cogito ergo sum* ('I think therefore I am') was *a priori*, that is arrived at by reasoning alone. Empiricist philosophers such as John Locke denied this, arguing that all knowledge was based on experience, i.e. is *a posteriori*.

The preposition *a, ab* (the latter when followed by a vowel) is always accompanied by a noun or adjective in the ablative case. The above three are examples of comparative adjectives: *fortior* is the comparative form of the adjective *fortis*, 'strong', so *fortior* is 'stronger'; similarly, *posterus*, 'next', yields the comparative *posterior*, 'later'; and *primus*, 'first', has the comparative *prior*, 'former'.

Note that although this ablative ending *-i* is typical of third declension adjectives, in good Classical usage the comparative adjective should have an ablative ending in *-e* (e.g. *priore anno*, 'in the previous year'). However, these phrases are late-Latin or medieval in origin, when the distinction was no longer so finely observed. Confusion is easily avoided, anyway, by remembering that *a, ab* always takes the ablative.

non sequitur

Speaking of *argumenta*, beware that any chain of reasoning could lead to a *non sequitur*. In English we treat it as a noun, as in 'that's a *non sequitur*', but actually it's a verb: *sequor* is a deponent verb, which is a grammatical term for a verb that looks passive but is in fact active: so instead of 'I am being followed' (passive) it means 'I follow' (active) – both literally in the sense of pursuing someone/thing and logically in the sense of following as a consequence, which is the meaning of our phrase. *Sequitur* is the third person singular ('he, she, it follows') plus the simple negative *non*.

CHAPTER 9

CHURCH LATIN

'Church Latin', sometimes known as 'Ecclesiastical Latin', is not some strange new language understood only by priests; it differs from Classical Latin in only a few respects:

- it changes some Classical syntax into something a little more like modern European languages, e.g. replacing the Classical accusative + infinitive construction for reported speech with phrases like *dixit ut* ..., 'he said that ...'
- it employs new words (many derived from Greek) and adapts the meaning of some old ones
- it is spoken with a slightly different pronunciation

It therefore reflects a natural development of the Latin language over the course of the centuries – from the high Classical period of the Augustan age to the declining years of the Roman Empire and the rise of the Christian Church.

PRONUNCIATION OF CHURCH LATIN

Preaching to the converted

Christians spread their message through preaching, often among the poor and illiterate classes, so inevitably they used the common speech (*sermo vulgaris*) that was familiar to their listeners, rather than the literary Classical Latin. St. Augustine wrote: 'I often employ words that are not Latin and I do so that you may understand me. Better that I should incur the blame of the grammarians than not be understood by the people.'

When spoken, Church Latin sounds rather like modern Italian (which is only a step away from Latin anyway). The main differences from Classical Latin are:

- u changes to ou – *Deus* is not *de-us* but *de-ous*
- c before e or i is not k but ch – *Cena* is not *ke-na* but *che-na*

- ti between two vowels is tsi – *Gratia* (hard t) becomes *gratsia*
- ti after a consonant (except s, t and x) is ci – *Roganti* becomes *roganci*
- g before e or i is soft, like j – *Gens* (hard g) becomes *jens*
- v is as in modern English, not the soft *w* of Classical pronunciation

A BRIEF HISTORY OF CHURCH LATIN

The rise of the Christian Church in the Roman Empire coincided with the decline of Classical Latin from the third century A.D. onwards. As the Empire became increasingly fragmented, ravaged by civil wars and continual strife on its borders, the tradition of Latin literature, too, began to wane. Few people had the leisure to compose new epic poetry or grandly conceived historical works. With the total loss of political freedom and the ever-present threat of disaster from external dangers, writers perhaps justifiably began to take a more introspective turn. Mysticism and Mystery Religions were more popular than ever. Plotinus (b. 205), for example, expounded a mystical philosophy – Neoplatonism – that denied the reality of the external world and exalted the soul's ascent to the spiritual realm of God. Though he lived and taught in Rome, Plotinus wrote in Greek. Despite the efforts of Cicero and Seneca centuries earlier, Greek had never been supplanted by Latin as the language of philosophical, religious and mystical speculation – even the Emperor Marcus Aurelius had written his famous *Meditations* in Greek.

St. Jerome (340-420)

Jerome (Latin *Hieronymus*) was born of a well-to-do Christian family in the province of Dalmatia. He was educated at Rome and later became famous for his asceticism. He admired pagan literature and quoted freely from Classical authors in his correspondence – even when he became a hermit he was unable to leave behind his library. Aside from his Vulgate Bible, Jerome also wrote biographies of eminent Christians and voluminous commentaries on Scripture.

Christians, too, used Greek. The original Christian liturgy was in Greek and the first

Christian writers wrote in Greek. The Old Testament was originally only known in the Greek version, the *Septuagint* (so-called because according to legend 72 Jewish scholars at Alexandria translated the original Hebrew in just 72 days). But by the fourth century, a Latin translation of the Bible was needed for the increasing number of converts in the Latin-speaking Western Roman Empire. However, in order to be understood as widely as possible, such a translation could not employ the formal, literary style of old Classical Latin.

Hence, the Latin Bible was to be written in the idiom of daily speech. St Jerome's Vulgate Bible (*vulgus*, 'common', 'popular') uses many colloquialisms and 'vulgar' words not found in earlier (aristocratic) Classical Latin. Jerome not only introduced new words into Latin (many borrowed from Greek), but also gave new meanings to some old words. For example:

Latin word	Classical meaning	Biblical meaning
conditor	founder	Creator
redemptor	buyer	Saviour
dominus	master	Lord

Other specifically Ecclesiastical Latin words include:

amen
> from Hebrew, via Greek. Can function as an adjective meaning 'true', 'faithful', but more generally as an adverb: 'faithfully', 'sincerely'

angelus
> from the Greek αγγελος, 'messenger'

annuntiatio
> 'an announcing' from late-Latin *adnuntio, adnuntiare*, 'to announce'

apostolus
> from the Greek αποστολος, 'sent', i.e. someone sent out on a special mission

baptisma

'a dipping in water' from Greek βαπτισμα, as is the verb *baptizo, baptizare.* Pliny the Younger calls a swimming pool a *baptisterium*

beatificus

a blessing, from *beatifico, beatificare,* 'to bless', derived from Classical *beatus facio,* literally 'make happy'

benedictus

from Classical *bene dicere,* 'to speak well [of someone]', so a *benedictus* is someone who has been spoken well of, 'blessed'

clerus

from the Greek κληρος, 'clergy'

consubstantialis

'of like nature or essence' – the Catholic creed holds that the Trinity is of one nature

ecclesia

from the Greek εκκλησια, an assembly of the people, so a Christian congregation, a church

episcopus

from the Greek επισκοπος, an 'overseer' or 'superintendent', hence a Bishop

evangelium

from the Greek ευαγγελιον, 'good news' (used in this sense by Cicero), hence the Gospel. Also the verb *evangelizo, evangelizare,* 'to bring good tidings', specifically preach the Gospel

incarnatio

from the verb *incarno, incarnare,* 'to make flesh', which in the passive is *incarnari,* 'to be made flesh', English 'incarnate'

martyr

> from the Greek μαρτυρ, 'witness'

nativitas

> for 'birth' Classical writers used *ortus* – 'a rising' hence 'beginning'
> – the perfect participle of *orior*, 'to rise' (present participle *oriens*,
> 'rising', hence English 'Orient')

peccator

> 'a sinner', from the verb *pecco, peccare*, 'to commit a fault, offend'
> – Classical writers used the present participle *peccans* to describe
> an offender

persecutor

> from the verb *persequor*, 'to follow after, pursue', in the Christian
> sense someone who doggedly pursues Christians – Classical
> writers used the present participle *persquens*, 'a pursuer'

sacramentum

> a technical legal term in Classical Latin referring to the sum of
> money which the two parties involved in a lawsuit deposited in
> a sacred place – the loser's money was used to pay for religious
> observances. It also referred to the first military engagement of
> new troops, who afterwards took the sacred oath of allegiance.
> So it came to mean the oath itself, i.e. something to be kept
> sacred

Jerome's *editio vulgata* was initially received with some hostility, but
gradually became accepted as the standard text of the Bible – with
various revisions over the centuries. It remains the official text of the
Roman Catholic Church.

A. SELECTIONS FROM THE VULGATE

1. *The Lord's Prayer*

Pater noster, qui es in caelis:
Sanctificetur nomen tuum.
Adveniat regnum tuum.

Fiat voluntas tua, sicut in caelo, et in terra.
Panem nostrum quotidianum da nobis hodie.
Et dimitte nobis debita nostra,
sicut et nos dimittimus debitoribus nostris.
Et ne nos inducas in tentationem.
Sed libera nos a malo.
Amen. (Matthew VI/9-13)

Notes:

1. pater noster – vocative, addressing 'our father', *qui es*, 'you who are ...', which sounds better in archaic English, 'Thou who art ...'

2. in caelis – ablative plural of *caelum*, 'heaven'

3. sanctificetur – passive subjunctive of *sanctifico, sanctificare*, 'sanctify', 'make holy', a Church Latin verb. Subjunctive because it expresses a desire or command: '*may/let* your name be made holy', passive because the subject 'your name' – *nomen tuum*, neuter – is to be made holy by the agency of others

4. Adveniat ... Fiat – both present subjunctive, expressing commands: '*Let* your kingdom come. *Let* your will be done ...', q.v. *Fiat lux* from *Genesis* below

5. in caelo – ablative singular

6. quotidianum – accusative agreeing with *panem nostrum*. Actually in the text of *Matthew*, Jerome uses the word *supersubstantialem*, 'necessary to support life', but *quotidianum*, 'daily' when the same phrase appears in *Luke* XI/3. *Quotidianum* is preferred when the prayer is printed on its own, and fits more with the familiar English translation, 'our daily bread'

7. da – imperative of *do, dare* followed by *nobis*, dative: 'give to us ...'

8. dimitte – imperative of *dimitto, dimittere*. q.v. *Exodus* below: *Dimitte populum meum*. The next line's *dimittimus* is the first person plural indicative. Basic meaning is 'send away', 'dismiss'; so in this context 'release from debt', i.e. 'forgive our debts'

9. *nobis* – dative because 'our debts' – *debita nostra*, neuter plural accusative – are being taken away *from* us

10. debitoribus nostris – the suffix *-tor* indicates a person: so *debitum* becomes *debitor* – just as in English a 'debt' becomes a 'debtor'. Dative plural because we are 'dismissing' those who are indebted to us

11. ne ... inducas – the indelible English translation 'Lead us not into temptation' looks like an imperative. The Latin *ne* + subjunctive (here of *induco, inducere*) is an alternative construction common

> in late-Latin where Classical Latin would prefer the negative
> imperative *noli, nolite*, 'don't' + infinitive, i.e. *noli inducere* (cf. *noli
> me tangere*)
> 12. libera – back to straightforward imperatives, this of *libero,
> liberare*
> 13. a malo – ablative

2. In the beginning ...

*In principio creavit Deus coelum et terram. Terra autem erat inanis et vacua,
et tenebrae erant super faciem abyssi: et Spiritus Dei ferebatur super aquas.
Dixitque Deus: Fiat lux, et facta est lux. Et vidit Deus lucem quod esset
bona: et divisit lucem a tenebris. Appellavitque lucem Diem, et tenebras
Noctem: factumque est vespere et mane, dies unus.* (Genesis I/1-5)

Notes:

1. principio – preposition *in* + ablative of *principium,* 'beginning'
2. creavit – perfect tense of *creo, creare,* 'create'
3. coelum et terram – accusatives, *caelum* is the more usual spelling
4. erat ... erant – imperfects of *sum, esse*
5. terra – nominative singular feminine, hence adjective *vacua* is
   feminine
6. *tenebrae* – nominative plural, but not 'darknesses' just 'darkness'
7. super – preposition + accusative plural of *aqua,* 'water'
8. ferebatur – imperfect passive of *fero, ferre,* 'bear', 'carry' – here
   'was moving', though English would normally just say 'moved'
   (perfect tense)
9. dixit – perfect tense of *dico, dicere*
10. fiat – subjunctive of *fio, fieri* to express a command, i.e. 'Let there
    be light'
11. facta est – perfect passive of *facio, facere*; feminine because *lux* is
    feminine
12. vidit – perfect tense of *video, videre*
13. lucem – accusative of *lux*
14. esset – imperfect subjunctive of *sum, esse*, subjunctive because
    it is the verb in a subordinate clause after quod ('that', where
    Classical Latin would proably use the accusative + infinitive
    construction)
15. bona – feminine because adjective agrees with the feminine
    noun *lux*
16. divisit – perfect tense of *divido, dividere*

17. tenebris – ablative plural of *tenebrae* (plural), following preposition *a, ab*

18. appellavit – perfect tense of *appello, appellare*

19. diem – accusative of *dies*, 'day'

20. noctem – accusative of *nox*, 'night'

21. factum est – perfect passive of *facio, facere* here used impersonally: 'it was made/done'

22. vespere – ablative, 'in the evening'

23. mane – not an ablative like *vespere* but an adverb, 'in the morning'

24. dies unus – nominative masculine, but not the subject of *factum est* (neuter), which would in that case be *factus est* (masculine). So *not* 'The first day was made in the morning and the evening'. The King James version has: 'And the evening and the morning were the first day'

3. *The plague of frogs*

Dixit quoque Dominus ad Moysen: Ingredere ad Pharaonem, et dices ad eum: Haec dicit Dominus: Dimitte populum meum, ut sacrificet mihi; Sin autem nolueris dimittere, ecce ego percutiam omnes terminos tuos ranis. Et ebulluiet fluvius ranas: quae ascendent, et ingredientur domum tuam, et cubiculum lectuli tui, et super stratum tuum, et in domos servorum tuorum, et in populum tuum, et in furnos tuos, et in reliquias ciborum tuorum: Et ad te, et ad populum tuum, et ad omnes servos tuos, intrabunt ranae.
(Exodus VIII/1-4)

Notes:

1. Much of this passage concerns what *will* happen, so there are several verbs in the future tense

2. dixit quoque – perfect tense, 'he also said', the Lord is delivering further instructions to Moses: *ad* + accusative *Moysen* – an example of the change in syntax: Classical Latin would put Moses in the dative then what the Lord had to say in the accusative with the verb in reported speech in the infinitive

3. ingredere – imperative of deponent verb *ingredior*, 'enter', 'approach'

4. Pharaonem – accusative following preposition *ad*

5. dices – our first future tense, 'you will say ...', of *dico, dicere*

6. eum – accusative of pronoun *is*, 'he', so *ad eum* = 'to him',

> another departure from Classical usage which would have used the dative *ei*

7. haec — accusative plural of neuter *hoc*, 'this', so 'these things'
8. dimitte — imperative of *dimitto, dimittere*
9. ut + subjunctive *sacrificet* (from *sacrifico, sacrificare*) is here a clause of purpose: 'so that they may sacrifice ...'
10. mihi — dative of personal pronoun *ego*, 'I'
11. sin — a conjunction, 'however', with *autem* 'but if'
12. nolueris — future perfect tense (perfect stem + future tense of *sum*) of *nolo, nolle* expressing something that will have been done in the future, literally and awkwardly in English: 'if you will not have wished ...'
13. dimittere — infinitive '... to release them'
14. ecce — an exclamation, 'behold!'; *ego* — the personal pronoun for emphasis: 'It is *I* who will ...'
15. percutiam — future tense of *percutio, percutere*
16. terminos tuos — accusative plural, 'your boundaries/borders'
17. ranis — ablative plural, 'with frogs'
18. ebulluiet — future tense of *ebullio, ebullire*, 'produce in abundance' (English 'ebullient')
19. ranas — accusative plural
20. quae — relative pronoun referring to the frogs so feminine, but nominative because it is the subject of the following verb *ascendent*
21. ascendent — future tense of *ascendo, ascendere* (English 'ascend')
22. ingredientur — future tense of deponent verb *ingredior* — there follows a list of all the places where the frogs will enter
23. domum tuam — *domus* is feminine, so accusative adjective *tuam* agrees
24. cubiculum — accusative, with *lectuli tui*, genitive: an odd phrase literally 'the bedroom of your bed', i.e. 'bedroom'
25. super — with accusative of neuter noun *stratum*, 'blanket'
26. servorum tuorum — genitive plural
27. in populum — *in* + accusative: 'into' or 'against' the people
28. reliquias ciborum tuorum — *reliquiae*, English 'relics' so 'leftovers'; *cibus*, 'food'
29. Et ad te — *ad* + accusative: 'towards', but better here 'upon'; *et ... et* 'both ... and'
30. intrabunt — future tense of *intro, intrare*. The King James version has 'And the frogs shall come up both upon thee, and upon thy people ...'

4. *And shepherds watched their flocks by night ...*   *

Et pastores erant in regione eadem vigilantes, et custodientes vigilias noctem
super gregem suum. Et ecce Angelus Domini stetit iuxta illos, et claritas
Dei circumfulsit illos, et timuerunt timore magno. Et dixit illis Angelus:
Nolite timere: ecce enim evangelizo vobis gaudium magnum, quod erit omni
populo: Quia natus est vobis hodie Salvator, qui est Christus Dominus in
civitate David. Et hoc vobis signum: Invenietis infantem pannis involutum,
et positum in praesepio. Et subito facta est cum Angelo multitudo militiae
caelestis laudantium Deum, et dicentium: Gloria in altissimis Deo, et in terra
pax hominibus bonae voluntatis. (Luke, II/8–14)

Notes:

1. pastores – nominative plural
2. erant – imperfect plural of *sum, esse*
3. in + ablative of *regio, regionis* (f); *eādem* (long *a*) is ablative of *eadem* (short *a*), feminine form of *idem*, 'the same'
4. vigilantes, custodientes – present participles of verbs *vigilo, vigilare* and *custodio, custodire*, both nominative plural in agreement with *pastores*: 'shepherds ... watching and guarding ...'
5. vigilias noctem – Latin uses the accusative to express time during which, as here: 'throughout the night watches'
6. super + accusative of *grex, gregis*, 'flock' (English 'gregarious'); *suum*, possessive adjective
7. ecce – exclamation, 'behold!', 'Lo!'
8. Domini – genitive
9. stetit – perfect tense of *sto, stare*
10. illos – 'them' accusative plural of *ille*, 'he'
11. Dei – genitive
12. circumfulsit – perfect tense of *circumfulgeo, circumfulgere*, 'shine around'
13. timuerunt – perfect tense of *timeo, timere*, 'fear' (verb); note alliteration with following *timore*, ablative of *timor, timoris*, 'fear' (noun)
14. dixit – perfect tense of *dico, dicere*
15. illis – 'to them', dative plural of *ille*
16. nolite timere – verb *nolo, nolle*, here in the imperative plural, is always followed by the infinitive
17. evangelizo – present tense, an Ecclesiastical Latin word. The King James Bible has the immortal line 'I bring you tidings of great joy'
18. vobis – dative plural, 'to you'

19. quod – relative pronoun neuter following *gaudium*, 'that which ...'
20. erit – future tense of *sum, esse*
21. omni populo – dative, 'to all people'
22. natus est – perfect tense of deponent verb *nascor*
23. Salvator – an Ecclesiastical word, Classical writers used *servator*
24. qui – relative pronoun telling us who is the *Salvator*
25. in + abative of *civitas, civitatis*
26. hoc ... signum – neuter
27. invenietis – future tense, 'you will find', second person plural, of *invenio, invenire*
28. pannis – ablative plural of *pannus*, 'a rag' (the 'swaddling clothes' of the King James version)
29. involutum ... positum – perfect passive participles of verbs *involvo, involvere* and *pono, ponere*, literally: 'having been wrapped' and 'having been placed'
30. in + ablative of neuter *praesepe*
31. subito – adverb
32. facta est – perfect passive of *facio, facere*, feminine because the nominative subject is feminine *multitudo*. Here 'created' or 'appeared'. The King James version treats it as synonymous with plain old 'was': 'And suddenly there was with the angel a multitude ...'
33. cum + ablative = 'with'
34. militiae caelestis – genitive: *militia*, 'military service' in Classical Latin but here 'the army' i.e. 'heavenly host'
35. laudantium ... dicentium – present participles of *laudo, laudare* and *dico, dicere*; genitive plural agreeing with *militiae coelestis* rather than nominative singular *multitudo*
36. altissimis – superlative, 'the highest', ablative following preposition *in*
37. Deo – dative 'to God'
38. et in terra pax hominibus bonae voluntatis – the King James Bible says 'and on earth peace, good will toward men', but the Latin syntax does not support this: *pax* – nominative, *hominibus* – dative plural: 'and on earth peace to men ...', but *bonae voluntatis* – genitive singular, '... of good will'

Thus, preserved in the form given to it in Jerome's Vulgate, Church Latin survived the downfall of the Western Roman Empire. It was further enriched by the Mass (see Chapter 10) and other liturgical hymns. All official documents issued by the Vatican are still written in Latin, and as late as 2005 Pope Benedict XVI chose to give his inaugural address in Latin:

B. VATICAN LATIN

1. '*Habemus Papam*'

Annuntio vobis gaudium magnum. Habemus Papam: Eminentissimum ac Reverendissimum Dominum, Dominum Josephum Sanctae Romanae Ecclesiae Cardinalem Ratzinger qui sibi nomen imposuit Benedicti Decimi Sexti

Notes:

1. annuntio – Church Latin for *adnuntio* (remember pronunciation: *annunt**s**io*)
2. vobis – dative plural, 'I announce *to you* ...'
3. gaudium magnum – accusative, *gaudium*, 'joy' is neuter. The phrase is a deliberate echo of *evangelizo vobis gaudium magnum* (Luke II/10 above)
4. Eminentissimum ... Reverendissimum – both superlative adjectives, accusative, agreeing with *Dominum Josephum*
5. Dominum – in the Vulgate, *Dominus* is always 'The Lord', but here the Classical 'master' seems more appropriate
6. Sanctae Romanae Ecclesiae – genitive: 'of the Sacred Roman Church'
7. qui sibi nomen imposuit – as with *mihi nomen est* (Chapter 2), literally 'he who upon himself has placed the name of ...'
8. Benedicti Decimi Sexti – genitive, following 'the name of ...'

Recommended reading:

St. Jerome (trans)   ***Biblia Sacra Vulgata* (The Vulgate Bible)**
                          Deutsche Bibelgesellschaft
                          Bible Society
Readers may prefer to track down a second-hand copy if possible.

J.F. Collins   ***A Primer of Ecclesiastical Latin***
                    CUA Press
A thorough introductory course in Church Latin.

L.F. Stelten (ed.)   ***A Dictionary of Ecclesiastical Latin***
                          Hendrickson Publishers Inc.
A useful dictionary of Church Latin.

CHAPTER 10

THE LATIN MASS

In chapters 10, 11 and 12 we will be looking at the central role of Latin in sacred music. From the early unaccompanied singing of liturgical Latin texts by choirs of monks, to the great works of composers such as Mozart and Beethoven, the history of Western music is inextricably intertwined with the Latin of Church ritual. The centrepiece of that ritual is the Mass.

ORIGIN OF THE MASS

The Christian celebration of the Eucharist is derived from Christ's example at the Last Supper as related in the New Testament. Originally the liturgy would have been in Greek, even at Rome, but between the second and sixth centuries Latin became the preferred language throughout the Western Roman Empire. Some Greek remains in the Mass, though, notably the opening invocation *Kyrie eleison*.

The Latin term for Mass, *Missa*, was first used by St Ambrose (d. 397). The word itself derives from the noun *missio, missionis*, 'a sending away', 'a dismissal', and originally referred only to the dismissal of the celebrants at the end of the service. Gradually *Missa* was applied to the whole liturgy. As well as giving rise to our English 'Mass', *Missa* is also the origin of 'Messe' (German), 'Messe' (French), 'Messa' (Italian) and 'Misa' (Spanish).

The Roman Mass consists of a series of individual poems of uncertain origin – some derived from earlier Greek or even Hebrew versions, others later additions. By the time of Pope Gregory the Great (590-604), the form of the Mass had been all but finalised. The earliest manuscripts still in existence date from the seventh century, and they present the Mass much as it is known today.

MUSIC AND THE MASS

From its earliest inception the Mass has been set to music, though

Neumes

The method of musical notation we have today was first developed for Gregorian Chant. This notation originally consisted of staves bearing lozenge shapes ('neumes') which provide the relative pitch of each note, but no specific indication of timing or tempo. Chants were collected into illuminated manuscripts called *Missals*.

until relatively recently it was always sung unaccompanied by any instruments.

1. *Plainchant*

Sung by monks for the daily Offices of the Church, Plainchant is often synonymous with Gregorian Chant, though there is also an alternative rite called Ambrosian Chant, named after St Ambrose who became Bishop of Milan in 374 and composed his own Latin hymns. The single melody of Plainchant is unadorned by any harmony, hence the 'plain' description, although the music is nonetheless often extremely florid. The Gregorian form takes its name from Gregory the Great, who is credited with promoting its use (unlike Ambrose he is not thought actually to have composed any of the music). In contrast to modern music there is no beat or regular accent to Gregorian Chant, and the actual pitch is not fixed so any piece can be sung to suit any voice. Chant melodies were written in a system of eight 'modes' (similar to but not the same as the modern major-minor key system) directly descended from those used by the ancient Greeks.

2. *Polyphony*

Gregorian Chant dominated Church music for centuries, but as the medieval period developed secular musical forms began to exert an influence. Plainsong melodies began to be ornamented with harmonies – composers adding separate parts for two, then three, four and more voices – ultimately to produce the kind of fully harmonised choral singing we know today.

The first complete polyphonic Mass whose composer can be identified was the *Messa de Nostre Dame* ('Mass of Our Lady') by Guillaume de Machaut (d. 1377). Other notable composers of poly-phonic Masses include Guillaume Dufay (1397-1474), Josquin des Prez

William Byrd (*c*.1539-1623)

The greatest English composer of his generation, William Byrd's English Anthems and keyboard music are still highly regarded today, but in his lifetime he was best known for his Latin music, including three Masses featuring the *Kyrie* for the first time in the English tradition, as well as his *Gradualia*, a complete setting of all the Propers for every feast day in the Roman Catholic liturgy.

(*c*.1455-1521) and Thomas Tallis (1505-1585) – the latter took polyphony as far as it would go with his massive setting of the motet *Spem in alium* for 40 voices. Italian composer Giovanni Pierluigi da Palestrina (*c*.1525-1594) wrote over 100 Masses including the *Missa Papae Marcelli*, one of the finest of all Mass settings.

But even during the heyday of Palestrina in the sixteenth century, the Mass was already in decline as *the* vehicle for composition. In the liturgical sphere, the smaller and more flexible Motet was being extensively used by composers such as Orlando de Lassus. After the Renaissance, secular music flourished: composers now freed from the constraints of writing only for the Church began to experiment with other musical forms, not only secular choral works but instrumental music and Opera.

Even so, some of the most famous of all musical works are Latin Masses: Bach's *B Minor Mass*, Mozart's *Mass in C minor* and his *Requiem Mass*, various settings by Haydn including his boisterous *Nelson Mass*, Beethoven's *Missa Solemnis* and Fauré's *Requiem* to cite just a handful of examples.

THE MASS ORDINARY AND PROPERS

The Latin Mass consists of the following individual pieces:
- Introit
- Kyrie
- Gloria
- Graduale
- Credo
- Offertory
- Sanctus
- Benedictus

- Agnus Dei
- Communion

These are commonly divided into two parts: the Ordinary and the Propers. The *Introit, Graduale, Offertory* and *Communion* texts are called the Propers because they are 'proper', i.e. specifically suitable, to a particular day or season (Christmas or Easter for example). The *Kyrie, Gloria, Credo, Sanctus, Benedictus* and *Agnus Dei* remain unchanged throughout, and are hence described as the Ordinary parts of the Mass, i.e. those parts ordinarily sung regardless of the specific occasion.

Usually, composers only set the Ordinary texts of the Mass to music, leaving the Propers to be performed as Plainchant. However, on certain specific occasions the Propers themselves are set to new music – a famous example being the *Requiem Mass* (Chapter 11).

THE MASS TEXTS (ORDINARY)

I. *Kyrie*

Kyrie eleison,
Christe eleison
Kyrie eleison.

Notes:
1. Kyrie – Greek noun, vocative of *Κυριος*, 'Lord'. A leftover from the original Greek liturgy
2. eleison – Greek verb, imperative of *ελειν*, 'have mercy'
3. Christe – vocative of *Christus*, Latin form of the Greek *Χριστος*

II. *Gloria*

Gloria in excelsis Deo
Et in terra pax hominibus bonae voluntatis.
Laudamus te, benedicimus te,
Adoramus te, glorificamus te,
Gratias agimus tibi propter magnam gloriam tuam,
Domine Deus, Rex caelestis,

Deus Pater omnipotens.

Domine Fili unigenite, Iesu Christe;

Domine Deus, Agnus Dei, Filius Patris.

Qui tollis peccata mundi, miserere nobis.

Qui tollis peccata mundi, suscipe deprecationem nostram.

Qui sedes ad dexteram Patris, miserere nobis.

Quoniam tu solus Sanctus, tu solus Dominus, tu solus Altissimus, Iesu Christe.

Cum Sancto Spiritu in gloria Dei Patris.

Amen

Notes:

1. For the first two lines see Chapter 9, extract 4

2. excelsis – ablative plural of *excelsus*, noun from verb *excello, excellere* (English 'excel')

3. laudamus ... benedicimus ... adoramus ... glorificamus – all present tense indicative; note poetical assonance

4. gratias agimus tibi – 'we give thanks to you' (see Chapter 2)

5. propter – 'because of', preposition + accusative

6. Domine – vocative, addressing God

7. caelestis – genitive singular of adjective *caelestis*, 'heavenly'

8. Domine Fili ... Iesu Christe – vocative, now addressing Jesus

9. unigenite – vocative of Ecclesiastical adjective *unigenitus*, 'only-begotten'

10. Agnus ... Filius – n.b. change from vocative to nominative

11. Dei ... Patris – genitive singulars

12. qui – relative pronoun nominative, take with *tollis*: 'you who take away ...', though old-fashioned 'Thou who takest away ...' sounds better

13. tollis – second person present tense of *tollo, tollere*

14. peccata – neuter accusative plural of *peccatum*, 'sin'

15. mundi – genitive singular of *mundus*, 'world' (English 'mundane')

16. miserere – imperative of *misereo, miserere*; *nobis* – dative plural, so: 'have mercy on us'

17. suscipe – imperative from *suscipio, suscipere*, 'accept, receive'

18. sedes – second person present tense of *sedeo, sedere* (English 'sedentary')

19. ad – preposition + accusative of *dextera, dexterae* (English 'dextrous')

20. tu solus Sanctus etc. – understand *est*

21. altissimus – superlative of *altus*
22. cum + ablative = 'with'
23. Sancto – ablative of second declension *Sanctus*; *Spiritu* ablative of fourth declension *Spiritus*
24. Amen – from the Hebrew word meaning 'so be it'

III. *Credo*

Credo in unum Deum, Patrem omnipotentem, factorem caeli et terrae, visibilium omnium et invisibilium.

Et in unum Dominum Iesum Christum, Filium Dei unigenitum.

Et ex Patre natum ante omnia saecula.

Deum de Deo, lumen de lumine, Deum verum de Deo vero.

Genitum, non factum, consubstantialem Patri, per quem omnia facta sunt.

Qui propter nos homines, et propter nostram salutem descendit de caelis.

Et incarnatus est de Spiritu Sancto ex Maria Virgine.

Et homo factus est.

Crucifixus etiam pro nobis sub Pontio Pilato, passus, et sepultus est.

Et resurrexit tertia die, secundum Scripturas.

Et ascendit in caelum, sedet ad dexteram Patris.

Et iterum venturus est cum gloria, iudicare vivos et mortuos, cuius regni non erit finis.

Et in Spiritum Sanctum Dominum, et vivificantem, qui ex Patre Filioque procedit.

Qui cum Patre, et Filio simul adoratur et conglorificatur, qui locutus est per Prophetas.

Et unam, sanctam, catholicam, et apostolicam Ecclesiam.

Confiteor unum baptisma in remissionem peccatorum.

Et expecto resurrectionem mortuorum.

Et vitam venturi saeculi.

Amen

Notes:

1. credo – when this verb is accompanied by a noun in the dative it means 'trust in', 'have confidence in'; but with the accusative as here it means 'believe', hence preposition *in* followed by accusative
2. patrem omnipotem ... factorem – accusatives agreeing with *Deum* after *credo*

3. caeli ... terrae – genitive singulars
4. visibilium omnium ... invisibilium – genitive plurals
5. et ... – more things 'I believe in', hence all accusative
6. ex Patre – preposition *ex* followed by ablative of *pater, patris*
7. natum – perfect participle of deponent verb *nascor*, 'born'
8. ante omnia saecula – preposition *ante* followed by accusative neuter plurals of *omnis* and *saeculum*
9. Deum de Deo etc. – accusative-preposition-ablative; translate *de* here as 'of' as in 'out of', 'from'
10. genitum – perfect passive participle from verb *gigno, gignere*, 'beget'; *factum* – perfect passive participle from verb *facio, facere*, 'make': so 'begotten not made'
11. consubstantialem – accusative, 'of like nature', a technical Ecclesiastical word, the source of much debate not to mention heresy in the early Church. *Patri* – dative
12. quem – accusative of pronoun *qui*, 'who' so 'whom'
13. facta sunt – perfect passive of *facio, facere*: '(they) are made'
14. qui – change now from accusatives, with 'I' as the subject to nominative *qui*, 'he who ...' explaining what 'He' has done
15. propter – preposition followed by accusative
16. descendit – perfect tense of *descendo, descendere* (English 'descend')
17. de – preposition followed by ablative plural
18. incarnatus est ... factus est ... sepultus est – all perfect passives, 'he was x and y and z', of *incarno, incarnare, facio, facere* and *sepelio, sepelire*
19. crucifixus – perfect passive participle of compound verb *crucifigo, crucifigere*, from ablative of *crux, crucis*, 'cross' and verb *figo*, 'fix', 'transfix'
20. passus – perfect participle active of deponent verb *patior*: 'he suffered'
21. resurrexit – perfect tense of *resurgo, resurgere* (English 'resurrect')
22. tertia die – ablative, the time when (see Chapter 5)
23. secundum – preposition, 'according to' + accusative of Ecclesiastical word *Scripturae*, 'Scriptures'
24. ascendit – perfect tense of *ascendo, ascendere* (English 'ascend')
25. sedet – shift to present tense, of *sedeo, sedere*
26. ad + accusative
27. venturus est – future passive of *venio, venire*: 'he will come (again) ...'
28. iudicare – infinitive of *iudico*
29. vivos et mortuos – accusative plurals, 'the quick and the dead'
30. cuius – genitive of pronoun *qui*: 'whose'; *regni* – genitive of *regnum*

31. erit – future tense of *sum, esse*, with *non*: 'it will not (end)'
32. et in Spiritum ... – back to the list of things in the accusative which 'I believe in ...'
33. vivificantem – present participle accusative of verb *vivifico, vivificare*, but here meaning 'giver of life', more properly *vivificator*, accusative *vivificatorem*
34. Patre Filioque – both ablative following *ex*
35. procedit – present tense of *procedo, procedere*
36. adoratur ... conglorificatur – passives of *adoro, adorare* and Ecclesiastical *conglorifico, conglorificare*, 'glorify together'
37. locutus est – perfect tense (not passive) of deponent verb *loquor*
38. confiteor – 'I confess', another deponent verb, active not passive
39. baptisma – neuter accusative, hence *unum*
40. peccatorum – genitive plural of *peccatum* (neuter); *mortuorum* – genitive plural of *mortuus*
41. venturi saeculi – genitives: future participle of *venio, venire* plus *saeculum*

IV. *Sanctus*

Sanctus, Sanctus, Sanctus, Domine Deus Sabaoth;
Pleni sunt coeli et terra gloria tua.
Hosanna in excelsis

Notes:
1. Domine – vocative
2. Sabaoth – Hebrew word for military hosts, so 'O Lord of hosts'
3. pleni – nominative plural of *plenus*, referring to *coeli et terra*
4. gloria tua – ablative, 'with your glory'
5. hosanna – Hebrew word: 'salvation has come'

V. *Benedictus*

Benedictus qui venit in nomine Domini.
Hosanna in excelsis.

Notes:
1. Benedictus – from the Classical *bene dicere* (see Chapter 9)

2.   qui – relative pronoun nominative with *venit*, third person present tense of *venio, venire*: 'he who comes ...'
3.   in + ablative of *nomen, nominis*
4.   Domini – genitive

VI. *Agnus Dei*

Agnus Dei, qui tollis peccata mundi, miserere nobis
Agnus Dei, qui tollis peccata mundi, dona nobis pacem.

Notes:
1.   A repeat of lines from the *Gloria* above, except:
2.   dona nobis pacem – *dona*, imperative of *dono, donare* (English 'donate'); *nobis* – dative; *pacem* – accusative of *pax, pacis*

Recommended listening:

There are many excellent recordings of the following works. In addition, Gregorian Chant recordings are also widely available, though I recommend getting a complete Mass setting rather than one of the non-liturgical Gregorian 'samplers'.

J.S. Bach	Mass in B minor
Beethoven	*Missa Solemnis* in D, Op. 123
Byrd	Masses for three, four and five voices
Haydn	*Missa in angustiis*, 'Nelson Mass'
Mozart	Mass in C minor, 'Great Mass'
Palestrina	*Missa Papae Marcelli*
Vivaldi	*Gloria* in D

CHAPTER 11

THE *REQUIEM MASS*

In Chapter 10 we examined the Ordinary of the Mass. In this chapter we turn our attention to the Propers – those parts of the liturgy used only on certain occasions – specifically the Propers for the Catholic Mass for the Dead, the famous *Requiem Mass*.

The *Requiem* derives its name from the first line of the Introit, *Requiem aeternam.* These words are inspired by a line from the apocryphal Fourth Book of Esdras (Ezra) in Jerome's Vulgate:

> *Expectate pastorem vestrum, requiem æternitatis dabit vobis ...*
> (Fourth Book of Esdras II/34)
> 'Await your shepherd, he will give eternal rest to you'

MUSICAL SETTINGS OF THE *REQUIEM*

Like other Masses, the *Requiem* was originally sung only as Plainchant. But the compelling subject-matter and the dramatic poetry of the text has long proved irresistible to composers. The first surviving polyphonic setting *c.*1460 is by Johannes Ockeghem (*c.*1410-1497); a setting by Antoine Brumel (*c.*1460-1515) was the first to include the *Dies iræ* Sequence.

The Council of Trent (1545-1563) prescribed the specific texts to be included in the *Requiem* – Mozart's famous setting uses this orthodox version. However, in more recent times many composers have chosen to set different texts, including the hymn *Libera me* (*libera*, imperative of *libero, liberare*), the motet *Pie Iesu* (*pie*, vocative of adjective *pius*), and the *In paradisum* from the Burial Service: for example, French composer Gabriel Fauré's lyrical *Requiem* (1888) substitutes the gentle *Pie Iesu* and *In paradisum* for the angry *Dies iræ* of the orthodox liturgy.

1. *Mozart and the Requiem*

The story of Mozart's *Requiem* has acquired the status of myth, especially following Peter Schaffer's treatment in his play and film *Amadeus* (1984). In July 1791, some six months before his death, a mysterious stranger approached the composer and commissioned a *Requiem Mass* from him. Already a sick man by then, Mozart became convinced that someone had poisoned him and ordered the *Requiem* to be ready in time for his own funeral service: 'It is for myself that I am writing this', he lamented. In fact, the commission was from dilettante composer Count Franz Walsegg-Stuppach, who had a penchant for passing off the works of 'proper' composers as his own – but Mozart didn't know this.

Mozart never completed the commission, whether because he feared he was hastening his own demise, or because he was working on the operas *Die Zauberflöte* and *La Clemenza di Tito* at the same time. The only parts of the work he fully scored were the *Requiem aeternam* and the *Kyrie eleison*. He made detailed sketches, including full vocal parts, for the Sequence as well as the Offertory. The very last thing he wrote was the first eight bars of the *Lacrimosa* – beyond that he could not go. He died on 5 December, 1791.

As the fee had been paid in advance, Mozart's widow Constanze had the work completed by his pupil Franz Xaver Süssmayr, whose version is the one best known today.

2. *The Requiem in the concert hall*

After Mozart, nineteenth-century *Requiems* moved the work from church to concert hall, being large-scale oratorios in all but name: *Requiems* by Rossini, Dvořák, Berlioz (*Grande Messe des Morts*) and Verdi are of this type. German-language settings by Schütz and Praetorius in the seventeenth century adapted the Catholic text to the Lutheran tradition, and their works inspired Brahms's famous *German Requiem* (1869).

In the twentieth century, Benjamin Britten's *War Requiem* (1962) mixed the Latin text with the poetry of Wilfred Owen. Polish texts are used by Krzysztof Penderecki (b. 1933) and Zbigniew Preisner (b. 1955) in their modern settings. Other recent versions include those by György Ligeti (b. 1923), Karl Jenkins (b. 1944) and Andrew Lloyd-Webber (b. 1948). This ancient and haunting sacred poetry continues and will always continue to fascinate composers and audiences alike.

THE *REQUIEM* – COMPLETE TEXT

I	Introitus: *Requiem aeternam*
II	Kyrie eleison★
III	Sequentia: *Dies iræ*
IV	Offertorium: *Domine Iesu*
V	Sanctus★
VI	Benedictus★
VII	Agnus Dei
VIII	Communio: *Lux aeterna*

★For the *Kyrie, Sanctus & Benedictus*, see Chapter 10

I. *Introitus*

Requiem aeternam dona eis, Domine,
et lux perpetua luceat eis.
Te decet hymnus, Deus, in Sion,
et tibi reddetur votum in Jerusalem.
Exaudi orationem meam,
ad te omnis caro veniet.
Requiem aeternam dona eis, Domine,
et lux perpetua luceat eis.

Notes:

1. requiem aeternam – accusatives
2. dona – imperative of *dono, donare*
3. eis – dative plural of pronoun *is, ea, id*; *Domine* – vocative, so 'give/grant to them eternal rest, O Lord'
4. perpetua – adjective agreeing with *lux*
5. luceat – present subjunctive, expressing a third-person wish/command: 'may/let perpetual light shine on them'
6. decet – impersonal verb, 'it is fitting' + accusative *te*
7. Deus – vocative
8. hymnus – noun, requires the verb to be supplied: 'it befits you that a hymn of praise [is sung] in Sion'
9. reddetur – future passive of *reddo, reddere*, neuter *votum* is the subject: 'a vow will be given back to you'
10. exaudi – imperative of *exaudio, exaudire*
11. veniet – future tense of *venio, venire*

III. *Sequentia*

The division into separate movements below are those of Mozart's setting, not part of the original poem.

(i) Dies iræ

Dies iræ, dies illa
solvet saeclum in favilla,
teste David cum Sibylla.

Quantus tremor est futurus
quando iudex est venturus
cuncta stricte discussurus.

Notes:
1. Note the triple rhyme scheme for each verse
2. iræ – genitive of *ira*; *illa* – pronoun, 'that'
3. solvet – future tense of *solvo, solvere*
4. saeclum – neuter accusative, 'the earth', hence 'secular' = 'earthly'
5. teste – ablative of *testis*, 'witness'
6. David ... Sibylla – ablatives: 'with David and the Sibyll bearing witness'. Both the Jewish David and the pagan Sibyll were held by Christians to have predicted the Last Judgement
7. futurus ... venturus ... discussurus – future participles of *sum, esse, venio, venire* and *discutio, discutere* – for poetical effect. *Discutio* in Classical Latin means 'shatter', 'shake', but it came to mean 'investigate'. Late-Latin uses the future participle to express purpose (the *ut* + subjunctive clause of Classical Latin), so translate *discussurus* as: 'to judge all things strictly'
8. cuncta – neuter accusative plural of adjective *cunctus, -a, -um*
9. stricte – adverb, 'strictly'

(ii) Tuba mirum

Tuba mirum spargens sonum
per sepulcra regionum
coget omnes ante thronum.

Mors stupebit et natura
cum resurget creatura
Iudicanti responsura.

Liber scriptus proferetur
in quo totum continetur,
unde mundus iudicetur.

Iudex ergo cum sedebit
quidquid latet apparebit,
nil inultum remanebit.

Quid sum miser tunc dicturus,
quem patronum rogaturus,
cum vix iustus sit securus?

Notes:

1. tuba – nominative, a trumpet not a tuba!
2. spargens – present participle, nominative, of *spargo, spargere*
3. mirum sonum – accusative
4. per + accusative plural of neuter *sepulchrum, sepulchri*
5. regionum – genitive plural of *regio, regionis*
6. coget – future tense of *cogo, cogere*
7. ante + accusative of *thronus, throni*
8. stupebit – future tense of *stupeo, stupere* (English 'stupefy')
9. resurget – future tense of *resurgo, resurgere*
10. creatura – a Church Latin word for 'Creation'
11. Iudicanti – present participle of *iudico, iudicare*, dative: 'to he who is judging' (often written with the medieval 'J')
12. responsura – future participle of *respondeo, respondere*, feminine in agreement with *creatura*. Again, the future participle to express purpose: 'to answer to the Judge'

Dies iræ

Attributed to Thomas of Celano (1190-1260), the *Dies iræ* is arguably the most famous and most evocative Medieval Latin poem. Like modern poetry, but unlike Classical models, the *Dies iræ* has rhymed line endings. It describes in vivid detail the Last Judgement, the summoning of the dead, the deliverance of the good and the damnation of the bad to eternal torment. It was adopted as the *Requiem* Sequence as early as the end of the fourteenth century, a position it held until the 1970 revision of the Roman Missal.

The ancient *Dies iræ* Plainchant melody has been used by several composers, including Berlioz (*Symphonie Fantastique*), Liszt (*Totentanz*) and Rachmaninoff (*Rhapsody on a Theme of Paganini, Isle of the Dead, Symphonic Dances*), and more recently has been quoted on many film soundtracks as diverse as *The Shining* and *Demolition Man*.

13. scriptus – passive perfect participle of *scribo, scribere*
14. proferetur – future passive of *profero, proferre*
15. in quo – relative pronoun, ablative, 'in which …'
16. continetur – present passive of *contineo, continere*
17. iudicetur – present passive subjunctive of *iudico, iudicare*
18. sedebit – future tense of *sedeo, sedere*
19. latet – present tense of *lateo, latere*
20. apparebit – future tense of *appareo, apparere*
21. remanebit – future tense of *remaneo, remanere*
22. dicturus … rogaturus – more future participles, of *dico, dicere* and *rogo, rogare*, take both with *sum*: 'what am I to say … to ask?'
23. quem … patronum – accusative: 'what advocate am I to ask [to defend me]'
24. vix – adverb, 'hardly'
25. cum + *sit*, subjunctive of *sum, esse*: 'since the just may hardly be secure'
26. iustus – substantive adjective (i.e. used as a noun); *securus* – adjective

(iii) Rex tremendae

Rex tremendae maiestatis,
qui salvandos salvas gratis,
salve me, fons pietatis.

Notes:

1. tremendae maiestatis – genitive
2. qui … salvas – verb *salvo, salvare*: 'you who save …'
3. salvandos – gerundive from *salvo, salvare*, literally: 'those who are to be saved', i.e. 'the redeemed'
4. gratis – adverb, 'freely'
5. salve – imperative of *salveo, salvere*
6. fons – vocative (a metaphorical description), with *pietatis* – genitive

(iv) Recordare

Recordare, Iesu pie,
quod sum causa tuae viae,
ne me perdas illa die.

Quaerens me sedisti lassus,
redemisti crucem passus,
tantus labor non sit cassus.

Iuste iudex ultionis
donum fac remissionis
ante diem rationis.

Ingemisco tamquam reus,
culpa rubet vultus meus,
supplicanti parce, Deus.

Qui Mariam absolvisti
et latronem exaudisti,
mihi quoque spem dedisti.

Preces meae non sunt dignae,
sed tu bonus fac benigne,
ne perenni cremer igne.

Inter oves locum praesta,
et ab haedis me sequestra,
statuens in parte dextra.

Notes:

1. recordare – imperative of deponent verb *recordor*
2. Iesu pie – vocative (q.v. *Pie Iesu*) of *pius*
3. quod – 'because'
4. tuae viae – genitive
5. ne + subjunctive *perdas* (of *perdo, perdere*) = 'Do not forsake me', a late-Latin construction equivalent to Classical Latin's *noli/ nolite* + infinitive
6. illa die – ablative of time
7. quaerens – present participle, nominative, of *quaero, quaerere*
8. lassus – 'weary' (English 'lassitude'); an allusion to John IV/6, *Jesus ergo fatigatus est ex itinere, sedebat sic supra fontem*: 'Jesus therefore being wearied with his journey, sat thus on the well' (King James translation)
9. sedisti ... redemisti – perfect tenses, second person singular ('you ...') of *sedeo, sedere* and *redimo, redimere* – Classical 'redeem' in

the sense of 'buy back', but for Christians the redemption of souls

10. lassus ... passus ... cassus – *lassus* and *cassus* are adjectives, *passus* is the perfect participle of deponent verb *patior*, used as an adjective

11. sit – subjunctive expressing a wish: 'let such toil not be in vain'

12. iuste – adverb, 'justly'

13. ultionis – genitive of *ultio*: 'judge of vengeance justly ... ' sense is completed by the next line

14. fac – imperative of *facio, facere*: literally 'make a gift of ...', so 'grant'

15. remissionis – genitive of *remissio*, Classical 'sending back', Ecclesiastical 'forgiveness'

16. rationis – genitive of *ratio*, 'reckoning'

17. reus – originally the defendant in a lawsuit, so 'a guilty man'

18. culpa – must be ablative not nominative, since *vultus meus* is nominative so: 'my face blushes with guilt'

19. parce – imperative of *parco, parcere*, takes dative hence *supplicanti*, dative of *supplicans*, 'one who is begging/imploring', present participle of verb *supplico, supplicare*

20. absolvisti ... exaudisti ... dedisti – perfect tenses, second-person singular, of *absolvo, absolvere, exaudio, exaudire* and *do, dare*

21. Mariam ... latronem – accusatives, of *Maria, Mariae* (Magdalene] and *latro, latronis*, 'robber'

22. mihi – dative of *ego*

23. spem – accusative of *spes, spei*

24. preces meae ... dignae – *dignus, -a, -um*, 'worthy of', usually takes the ablative in Classical Latin but here it agrees with noun *preces*

25. bonus – nominative with *tu*: literally 'good you', but here 'you who are kind/merciful' (as ever, archaic 'Thou who art ...' captures it better)

26. fac – imperative: 'make' or 'grant'; *benigne* – adverb, 'benevolently', from adjective *benignus, -a, -um* (English: 'benign')

27. ne + passive subjunctive of *cremo, cremare* = purpose clause: 'in order that I may not burn ...'

28. perenni ... igne – ablatives, *ignis* is the noun

29. praesta – imperative of *praesto, praestare*: 'show (me)'

30. locum – 'show me' what? a place (accusative) 'among the sheep' (*oves*, accusative plural of *ovis*)

31. ab haedis – ablative plural of *haedus*, strictly a young goat, a kid (*caper, capri* = male-goat; *capra, caprae* = she-goat)

32. sequestra – imperative of *sequestro, sequestrare*, 'separate' (English 'sequester')
33. statuens – present participle of *statuo, statuere*: 'standing (me) ...'
34. in parte dextra – 'on the right side'

(v) Confutatis

Confutatis maledictis
flammis acribus addictis,
voca me cum benedictis.

Oro supplex et acclinis,
cor contritum quasi cinis,
gere curam mei finis.

Notes:

1. confutatis maledictis – ablative absolute construction: *confutatis* is perfect passive participle of *confuto, confutare*, 'reproach, put to silence'; *maledictis* – ablative plural of *maledictus*, a late-Latin adjective here used as a noun (Classical Latin *exsecrabilis* – English 'execrable'): 'When the damned have been confounded ...'
2. flammis ... addictis – *addictis*, ablative perfect participle passive of *addico, addicere*, 'sacrifice', in agreement with *maledictis*; followed by the dative of noun *flamma, flammae* – 'blaze, flame' and its adjective *acer, acris*, 'sharp, bitter', so 'sacrificed to the bitter flames'
3. voca – imperative of *voco, vocare*
4. cum + ablative plural of *benedictus*
5. supplex – nominative: 'As a suppliant I beg ...'
6. acclinis – another adjective, originally 'leaning on/against', later 'inclined/disposed to'. Translate here as 'kneeling' (Classical *genibus*, from *genu*, 'knee', hence English 'genuflect')
7. contritum – adjective with neuter accusative *cor*, actually perfect participle passive of *contero, conterere*. Classical 'grind, bruise', late-Latin 'grief, contrition' – so 'a contrite heart'
8. gere – imperative of *gero, gerere*: literally 'have the care of my end', so 'safeguard my end'

(vi) Lacrimosa

Lacrimosa dies illa
qua resurget ex favilla
iudicandus homo reus.
huic ergo parce, Deus,
Pie Iesu Domine,
dona eis requiem.

Notes:

1. These six lines are a later addition to the *Dies iræ* poem – they use rhymed couplets not triplets, while the final two lines lack a syllable and do not rhyme but rely on assonance (similarity of sound)
2. lacrimosa ... illa – agreeing with noun *dies*
3. qua – ablative introducing a relative clause: 'the day on which ...'
4. resurget – future tense of *resurgo, resurgere*
5. iudicandus – gerundive, a passive adjective from the verb *iudico, iudicare*, 'judge': so 'the guilty man (who is) to be judged'
6. parce – imperative of *parco, parcere*, 'spare', takes the dative hence *huic*, dative of pronoun *hic*
7. Deus – vocative
8. Pie Iesu Domine – vocative
9. dona – vocative of *dono, donare*; *eis* – dative plural of pronoun *is*

IV. *Offertorium*

(i) Domine Iesu

Domine, Iesu Christe, Rex gloriae,
libera animas omnium fidelium defunctorum
de poenis inferni, et de profundo lacu:
libera eas de ore leonis,
ne absorbeat eas tartarus, ne cadant in obscurum,
sed signifer sanctus Michael
repraesentet eas in lucem sanctam,
quam olim Abrahae promisisti
et semini eius.

Notes:

1. libera – imperative of *libero, liberare*
2. animas – accusative plural of *anima, animae*
3. omnium ... defunctorum – all genitive 'of all the faithful departed'; *defunctorum* is the perfect participle active of deponent verb *defungor*
4. poenis – ablative (following preposition *de*) of *poena, poenae*
5. inferni – genitive singular of *infernus*, the Classical lower world, Christian 'Hell'
6. profundo – ablative of *profundus*; *lacu* – ablative of *lacus* – 'deep lake', but 'bottomless pit' fits better with ideas of Hell
7. eas – accusative plural of pronoun *ea*, feminine because referring to the *animas*: 'those souls'
8. ore – ablative of *os, oris*, 'mouth' (English 'oral')
9. leonis – genitive of *leo*
10. ne + present subjunctive of *absorbeo, absorbere* = a negative command (an alternative to the imperative): 'let not tartarus swallow them up'
11. ne ... ne – 'neither ... nor ...'
12. tartarus – in Classical mythology the infernal region
13. ne + subjunctive of *cado, cadere*, 'kill', in the third person = another negative command
14. in + accusative of neuter *obscurum* – 'into darkness'
15. signifer – nominative, 'standard-bearer'
16. repraesentet – present subjunctive of *repraesento, repraesentare* expressing a command: 'let St Michael bring them back ...'
17. in lucem sanctam – *in* + accusatives = 'into'
18. quam – relative pronoun agreeing with *lucem sanctam*: 'which ... '
19. Abrahae – dative of *Abraham*
20. promisisti – second person singular, perfect tense of *promitto, promittere*
21. semini – dative of *semen*, 'seed' so 'offspring, descendants'

(ii) Hostias

Hostias et preces, tibi, Domine,
laudis offerimus:
tu suscipe pro animabus illis,
quarum hodie memoriam facimus:
fac eas, Domine, de morte transire ad vitam,
quam olim Abrahae promisisti
et semini eius.

Notes:

1. hostias ... preces – accusative plurals of *hostia, hostiae* and *prex, precis*: 'offerings and prayers'
2. tibi – dative of *tu*
3. laudis – genitive of *laus*: 'of praise' or 'of worth', so 'well-deserved'
4. suscipe – imperative of *suscipio, suscipere*
5. pro + ablative plural of *anima* and *illa*: 'for [the sake of] those souls'. Irregular form *animabus* to distinguish the feminine from the masculine *animis*: other examples include *dea*, ablative *deabus* and *filia*, ablative *filiabus*
6. quarum – relative pronoun, genitive feminine plural agreeing with *animabus*: 'of which ...'
7. facimus memoriam – literally 'we make a memory' so 'commemorate'
8. fac – imperative of *facio, facere*: 'grant'
9. de + ablative of *mors, mortis*: 'from ...'; *ad* + accusative of *vita, vitae*: 'to[wards] ...'
10. transire – infinitive of *transeo*
11. quam ... eius – see *Domine Iesu* above

VII. *Agnus Dei*

Agnus Dei, qui tollis peccata mundi,
dona eis requiem.
Agnus Dei, qui tollis peccata mundi,
dona eis requiem sempiternam.

Notes:

1. See Chapter 10 for notes on *Agnus Dei* ...; Introit (above) for *dona eis requiem*
2. sempiternam – accusative adjective of *sempiternus, -a, -um*, 'everlasting'

VIII. *Communio*

Lux aeterna luceat eis, Domine,
cum sanctis tuis in aeternum,
quia pius es.
Requiem aeternam dona eis, Domine,
et lux perpetua luceat eis,

cum sanctis tuis in aeternum,
quia pius es.

Notes:

1. aeterna – adjective agreeing with *lux*
2. luceat – present subjunctive, same construction as in the Introit
3. cum + ablative plural of *sanctus*, 'holy', so literally 'your holy [ones]', i.e. 'Saints'
4. in + accusative of *aeternus*: 'into eternity' so 'for ever'

Recommended listening:

As mentioned above, many great composers have set the Latin *Requiem* text. Here are only a few recommendations, all available on CD:

Mozart	*Requiem* in D minor (1791)
Berlioz	*Grande Messe des Morts* (1837)
Verdi	*Messa da Requiem* (1868)
Fauré	*Requiem* in D minor (1888)

CHAPTER 12

LATIN CHRISTMAS CAROLS & HYMNS

It's not just the lengthy Mass that has received the attention of composers over the centuries. Thanks to memorable musical settings, many Latin hymns and carols remain staples of the concert-hall and popular repertoire. In this chapter we will examine just a few famous examples.

A. CHRISTMAS CAROLS

The exact origin of Christmas carols is unknown: St Francis of Assisi is traditionally credited with inventing them in the thirteenth century – or at least giving the pre-existing folk dances and songs called 'carols' religious respectability by performing them in the context of a Christian nativity scene.

1. *Adeste fideles*

Carol

The derivation of the word 'carol' is uncertain, but it may come from the French *caroller*, a circle dance, in turn from the Latin *choraules*, a choral dance accompanied by flute, itself a Latinised form of the same word in Greek.

Not a traditional carol at all, *Adeste fideles* was written by Englishman John Francis Wade (*c.*1710-1786) – a Jacobite exile who collected Latin music for the Catholic Church – and published in a selection of his own Latin hymns, *Cantus Diversi* in 1751. The song did not make much of an impression back in his native country until it was translated into English as 'O Come All Ye Faithful' by Frederick Oakely in 1841. But by then its origin had been forgotten: it was called the Portuguese Hymn following a performance at the Portuguese Embassy in London; and in 1860 organist Vincent Novello thought it was by a contemporary named John Redding. It was even attributed to thirteenth-century St Bonaventura.

Adeste, fideles, laeti triumphantes;
venite, venite in Bethlehem.
natum videte Regem angelorum.
Venite adoremus, Dominum.

Deum de Deo, Lumen de Lumine,
gestant puellae viscera;
Deum verum, genitum non factum:
Venite adoremus, Dominum.

Cantet nunc hymnos chorus angelorum;
cantet nunc aula caelestium:
Gloria in excelsis Deo!
Venite adoremus Dominum.

Ergo qui natus die hodierna,
Iesu, tibi sit gloria;
Patris aeterni verbum caro factum.
Venite adoremus, Dominum.

Notes:

1. adeste – imperative plural of *adsum, adesse*: 'be present' or more famously 'O come ...', though more correctly 'come' is *venite* in the next line
2. fideles – who should be come? vocative, plural of *fidelis*, i.e '(ye) faithful'
3. laeti ... triumphantes – how should they come? *laeti* – nominative plural of adjective *laetus*; *triumphantes* – present participle nominative plural of *triumpho, triumphare*: 'happy, triumphant'
4. venite – imperative plural of *venio, venire*
5. in + accusative = 'to(wards)'
6. videte – imperative plural of *video, videre*
7. natum ... regem – come to see what? *natum* – 'born', accusative of perfect participle of deponent verb *nascor*; *regem* – 'king', accusative of *rex, regis*; *angelorum* – genitive plural of *angelus*
8. adoremus – present subjunctive of *adoro, adorare*: 'let us adore ...'

9. Deum ... Lumine – a line from the *Credo* of the Mass (see Chapter 10)

10. gestant – plural of *gesto, gestare* – late-Latin alternative for *fero* or *porto*, plural because *viscera* is subject; *puellae* – genitive singular; *viscera* – neuter plural nominative: 'the womb of the girl carries ...' – a late-Latin usage, as Classical Latin for 'womb' is, unsurprisingly, *uterus* (*viscera* meant internal organs)

11. Deum ... factum – another quote from the *Credo*

12. cantet – present subjunctive of *canto, cantare*: 'let x sing'; subjects are (a) *chorus angelorum* then (b) *aula caelestium*

13. Gloria ... Deo – another quote from the Mass (originally from the Vulgate)

14. die hodierna – ablative of time: 'on this very day'

15. Iesu – vocative; *tibi* – dative; *sit* – present subjunctive of *sum, esse*: literally: 'let there be glory to you, O Jesus ...'

16. patris aeterni – genitive; *verbum* – neuter nominative, with *factum*, 'made'; *caro* – 'flesh', what 'the word of the eternal father' was made into

2. *Personent hodie*

A medieval carol, *circa* twelfth century, *Personent hodie* is sung by a choir of men and boys as a processional on the Feast of the Holy Innocents, 28 December, the commemoration of the slaughter of the innocents by King Herod. The carol was set in 1916 by Gustav Holst (1874-1934), whose arrangement has proved enduringly popular.

Personent hodie voces puerulae,
laudantes iucunde Qui nobis est natus,
summo Deo datus,
et de virgineo ventre procreatus.

In mundo nascitur, pannis involvitur
praesipi ponitur stabulo brutorum,
Rector supernorum.
Perdidit spolia princeps infernorum.

Magi tres venerunt, parvulum inquirunt,
Bethlehem adeunt, stellulam sequendo,

ipsum adorando,
aurum, thus et myrrham ei offerendo.

Omnes clericuli, pariter pueri,
cantent ut angeli: advenisti mundo,
laudes tibi fundo.
Ideo gloria in excelsis Deo.

Notes:

1. personent – present subjunctive: 'Let [them] resound ...'
2. voces – nominative plural of *vox, vocis; puerulae* – genitive of diminutive adjective *puerulus, -a, -um*: 'boyish voices'. Medieval Latin often uses the diminutive where Classical Latin would not (the Classical adjective 'boyish' is *puerilis*, English 'puerile')
3. laudantes – present participle of *laudo, laudare;* iucunde – adverb, 'joyously'
4. qui ... est natus – 'he who is born; *nobis* – dative plural, 'to us'
5. summo Deo – ablative; *datus* – perfect passive participle of *do, dare:* 'given by the highest God [God on high]'
6. de + ablative of *venter, ventris* and adjective *virgineus; procreatus* – the last of three rhyming perfect participles, of *procreo, procreare:* 'begotten'
7. in + ablative of *mundus*
8. nascitur ... involvitur – active, of deponent verb *nascor;* and passive of active verb *involvo, involvere*
9. pannis – ablative plural of *pannus*, 'rag' (see Chapter 9: Luke, II/8-14)
10. praesipi ... stabulo – both ablative, translate as 'in ...'; variant spelling of *praesaepi*, ablative of neuter *praesaepe* (variant *praesepe*); *stabulo* from *stabulum*, with *brutorum* – genitive plural of *brutus*
11. ponitur – passive of *pono, ponere*
12. Rector – add suffix *-tor* to *rectus*, perfect passive participle of verb *rego, regere; supernorum* – genitive plural of *supernus*
13. perdidit – perfect tense of *perdo, perdere:* subject is *princeps infernorum* (genitive of *infernus*); *spolia* – accusative neuter plural (English 'spoils')
14. venerunt – perfect tense of *venio, venire:* subject is the *tres Magi*
15. inquirunt – present tense from *inquiro;* whom are they seeking? *parvulum* – accusative of diminutive noun *parvulus*
16. adeunt – present tense from *adeo*

17. stellulam – accusative of diminutive noun *stellula*: another diminutive where Classical Latin would use the simple noun *stella*, 'star'

18. sequendo ... adorando ... offerendo – all gerunds, ablative (1) from deponent verb *sequor*; (2) from *adoro, adorare*; (3) from *offero, offerre* – 'by following ...', 'adoring' and 'offering' – though in Medieval Latin usage the ablative gerund often does the job of the Classical present participle, so the translation could simply be 'following ... adoring ... offering' (Classical *sequentes ... adorantes ... offerentes* – nominative plural agreeing with *Magi*)

19. aurum, thus, myrrham – all accusative; *ei* – dative of pronoun *is*

20. omnes clericuli ... pueri – nominative; *clericuli* is another diminutive ('little clerics') that need not be translated literally

21. pariter – adverb, 'equally'

22. cantent – present subjunctive of *canto, cantare*; ut – 'as' or 'like'

23. advenisti – perfect tense of *advenio, advenire*; *mundo* – dative of *mundus*

24. fundo – present tense; *laudes* – accusative plural of *laus*; *tibi* –dative

25. ideo – adverb, 'therefore'

26. gloria in excelsis Deo – see *Gloria* of the Mass (see Chapter 10)

3. *Quem pastores laudavere*

A Medieval Latin carol of German origin, this belongs to a type of song known as *Wechselgesänge* (antiphonal songs). Note the clever construction which delays the key verb *resonet*: normal prose word-order would begin with the final verse: 'Let "Praise, honour and glory" resound ...'

Quem pastores laudavere,
quibus angeli dixere:
'Absit vobis iam timere:
Natus est Rex Gloriae!'

Ad quem magi ambulabant,
aurum, thus, myrrham portabant;
immolabant haec sincere
Leoni victoriae;

Christo Regi, Deo nato,
per Mariam nobis dato,
merito resonet vere:
'Laus, honor, et gloria!'

Notes:

1. quem – accusative of *qui*: 'he whom ...'
2. laudavere – alternative form of *laudaverunt*, third-person plural perfect of *laudo, laudare*
3. quibus – relative pronoun referring to the shepherds, dative plural, 'to whom'
4. dixere – alternative form of *dixerunt*, third-person plural perfect of *dico, dicere*
5. absit vobis ... timere – literally: 'let it be absent from you [to] fear': *absit* – present subjunctive of *absum, abesse*; *vobis* – personal pronoun, dative plural; *timere* – infinitive of verb *timeo*. Equivalent to Classical phrase *nolite timere*, 'don't be afraid'
6. natus est – perfect tense of deponent verb *nascor*
7. ad + accusative = 'towards'; *ambulabant ... portabant ... immolabant* – imperfects of *ambulo, ambulare, porto, portare* and *immolo, immolare* (English 'immolation')
8. aurum, thus, myrrham – accusatives of *aurum* ('gold'), *thus* ('frankincense') and *myrrha* ('myrrh')
9. haec – neuter plural accusative of *hoc*, 'these things'; *sincere* – adverb, 'sincerely'
10. leoni – dative of *leo, leonis* (the person to whom 'these things' are being offered); *victoriae* – genitive of *victoria*
11. Christo Regi – dative following *Leoni*; *Deo nato ... dato* – also dative, agreeing adjectivally (*nato* perfect participle of deponent verb *nascor*; *dato* perfect participle passive from *do, dare*); *nobis* – also dative, with *dato*: 'given to us'
12. merito ... vere – adverbs: 'deservedly ... truly', translate together as 'right worthily'
13. resonet – present subjunctive, the main verb of the whole carol; *laus, honor, gloria* – nominative, the subjects of the poem (Christ is the object *quem* in the first line)

B. HYMNS

The Classical Latin word for 'song' is *carmen, carminis* (neuter, third declension). But the secular *carmina* of the Roman poets were associated by Christians with much that was deemed worldly, lascivious and indecent, so they adopted a more sober word to describe their pious practice of singing praises to God. *Hymnus, hymni* (masculine, second declension) is derived, like so many other Christian-Latin words, from a Greek original: ὕμνος.

1. *Ave Maria*

Not strictly speaking a hymn at all, the *Ave Maria* is a prayer addressed to the Virgin Mary that concludes with a plea for her intercession on the suppliant's behalf. Although not officially incorporated into Catholic liturgy until the fifteenth century, versions of the *Ave Maria* existed long before. The popularity of prayers and hymns addressed to Mary is summed up by F.J.E. Raby:

Only by recourse to a woman's pity could the medieval imagination find a hope of robbing the terrible day of judgement of part at least of that terror which pressed so heavily upon the soul. In the later Middle Ages ... Mary takes her place above all the saints as the most powerful agent of human succour: no prayers would weary her, her mercy and her might were alike unbounded. (*A History of Christian-Latin Poetry*)

Schubert's *Ave Maria*

Franz Schubert's setting remains the most famous, though Schubert didn't actually set the Latin text at all: his original song was a German translation of an excerpt from Sir Walter Scott's poem *The Lady of the Lake*, in which the heroine Helen prays to the Virgin. It is not known who first chose to sing the old Latin prayer to Schubert's melody, but ever since this has been the version most performed.

The *Ave Maria* takes its inspiration from the passage in the Vulgate where the Angel Gabriel descends to tell Mary of her destiny:

Et ingressus Angelus ad eam dixit: Ave gratia plena: Dominus ecum: Benedicta tu in mulieribus (Luke I/28)

And the angel being come in, said unto her: Hail, full of grace: the Lord is with thee: Blessed art thou among women.

Ave Maria, gratia plena, Dominus tecum.
Benedicta tu in mulieribus,
et benedictus fructus ventris tui, Iesus.
Sancta Maria, Mater Dei,
ora pro nobis peccatoribus, nunc,
et in hora mortis nostrae.
Amen.

Notes:

1.   ave – 'hail' (see Chapter 2: Conversational Latin)
2.   plena – adjective agreeing with *gratia*
3.   tecum – a compound word *te* (ablative of *tu*) + *cum* (takes ablative). Supply *est* here and also for the following two lines
4.   benedicta – feminine adjective agreeing with *Maria*
5.   in mulieribus – ablative plural of *mulier*: 'among women'
6.   benedictus – masculine agreeing with *Iesus*
7.   ventris tui – genitive of *venter* + possessive adjective *tuus*
8.   sancta – feminine agreeing with *Maria*
9.   dei – genitive of *deus*
10. ora – imperative of *oro, orare* (English 'oration', 'orator')
11. pro nobis peccatoribus – preposition *pro* + ablative plural of *peccator* and plural pronoun *nos*: 'on behalf of we sinners'
12. in + ablative of *hora, horae*
13. mortis nostrae – genitive of *mors* + possessive adjective *noster*

2. Stabat Mater

'A supreme achievement of the Franciscan, and, indeed, of the religious verse of the Middle Ages,' (F.J.E. Raby) the *Stabat Mater* has been variously attributed to Jacopone da Todi (*c.*1228-1306), Pope Innocent III (*c.*1160-1216) and St Bonaventura (d. 1274), but its authorship remains unknown for certain. The poem's vivid depiction of and sensitive empathy with the sufferings of a mother at the feet of her dying son has inspired many composers over the centuries.

Stabat Mater dolorosa,
iuxta crucem lacrimosa,
dum pendebat Filius.

Cuius animam gementem,
contristantem et dolentem,
pertransivit gladius.

O quam tristis et afflicta
Fuit illa benedicta
Mater Unigeniti.

Quae maerebat et dolebat,
et tremebat cum videbat
nati poenas incliti.

Plainchant poetry

The *Stabat Mater*, like the great *Dies iræ* of the *Requiem*, is a poem designed to be sung – originally as Plainchant by choirs of monks. Each of the 20 stanzas has three lines; while each pair of stanzas rhymes in the pattern AAB CCB. Try reading the poem aloud to get the full effect of the rhythmic word-setting.

Notes for stanzas 1-4:

1. stabat – imperfect of *sto, stare*. The imperfect tense provides an almost cinematic sense of the action happening in front of us
2. dolorosa ... lacrimosa – 'sorrowful ... weeping', adjectives agreeing with *mater*
3. iuxta – preposition + accusative of *crux, crucis* (hence 'crucify')
4. pendebat – another vivid imperfect tense, of *pendeo, pendere*; *Filius* – nominative, the subject of the verb
5. cuius – genitive of relative pronoun *qui*. Some translations give the subject as Mary – 'her lamenting heart' – but preceding clause subject is *Filius*, thus it seems equally possible to read: 'while her Son was hanging, the sword pierced his heart ... '
6. gementem ... contristantem ... dolentem – present participles accusative of *gemo, gemere, contristo, contristare* and *doleo, dolere*: 'lamenting ... sorrowing ... grieving'
7. pertransivit – perfect tense of compound verb *per-transeo, per-transire*, 'go through', 'pierce'. Note poetical effect: the vivid tenses of imperfect (*stabat ... pendebat*) and present (*gementem ...*) are brought to a sudden stop with this perfect, delayed until the end of the six-line rhyme scheme
8. gladius – nominative
9. O quam – a new six-line section begins, the subject is *mater* (line 9)
10. tristis ... afflicta ... benedicta – adjectives agreeing with *mater*
11. unigeniti – genitive of Ecclesiastical adjective *unigenitus*

12. quae — relative pronoun, feminine agreeing with *mater*, nominative because subject of the next four verbs

13. maerebat ... dolebat ... tremebat ... videbat — more vivid imperfects: from *maereo, maerere* (sometimes spelt *moerebat*), *doleo, dolere, tremo, tremere* and *video, videre*

14. poenas — accusative plural of *poena, poenae*

15. nati ... incliti — genitives: *natus* (participle from deponent verb *nascor*), 'born', used as a substantive, i.e. 'son'

Quis est homo qui non fleret
Christi Matrem si videret
in tanto supplicio?

Quis non posset contristari,
Piam Matrem contemplari
dolentem cum Filio?

Pro peccatis Suae gentis
vidit Iesum in tormentis,
et flagellis subditum.

Vidit suum dulcem natum
morientem desolatum
dum emisit spiritum.

Notes for stanzas 5-8:

1. fleret ... videret — more imperfect tenses, this time subjunctives of *fleo, flere* and *video, videre*, asking a rhetorical question beginning with *quis est*: 'who is the man who would not ...?', better: 'Is there any man who ...?'

2. in + ablative of neuter *supplicium* with adjective *tantus*

3. posset — imperfect subjunctive of *possum, posse* followed by infinitive

4. contristari ... contemplari — infinitives: passive of *contristo, contristare* (already encountered as *constristantem*) – 'who would not be sad' – and active of deponent verb *contemplor*

5. cum + ablative of *Filius* = 'with the Son'

6. pro + ablative plural of *peccatum*

7. suae – genitive of possessive pronoun; *gentis* – genitive of *gens*

8. vidit – perfect tense of *video, videre*. Subject is Mary. Perfect

      tense because we are now looking back at events that happened
      before the crucifixion

9.   in + ablative plural of neuter *tormentum* (English 'torment')
10. subditum – perfect passive participle of *subdo, subdere*: literally 'having been subjected to ...'; hence *flagellis* – dative plural
11. dulcem – accusative of adjective *dulcis*, with *suum ... natum*
12. morientem – present participle accusative of deponent verb *morior*
13. desolatum – perfect participle passive of *desolo, desolare*: '[having been] forsaken'
14. emisit – perfect tense of *emitto, emittere* (English 'emission')

Eia Mater, fons amoris,
me sentire vim doloris,
fac, ut tecum lugeam.

Fac, ut ardeat cor meum
in amando Christum Deum,
ut sibi complaceam.

Sancta Mater, istud agas,
crucifixi fige plagas
cordi meo valide.

Tui nati vulnerati,
tam dignati pro me pati
poenas mecum divide.

Notes for stanzas 9-12:

1. The perspective now changes as the poet directly addresses Mary and asks to participate with her suffering
2. eia – an exclamation – 'oh!' – in Classical Latin more commonly used to express joy
3. amoris – genitive of *amor*
4. me ... fac – English word order is: *fac me sentire vim doloris. fac* – imperative with s*entire* – infinitive; *vim* – accusative of *vis*; *doloris* – genitive of *dolor*: 'make me feel the force of your sorrow'
5. ut + subjunctive of *lugeo, lugere* = 'in order that I may mourn ...'

6. ut + subjunctive of *ardeo, ardere* (English 'ardent') = 'in order that my heart may burn/glow ...'

7. *amando* – ablative gerund of verb *amo, amare* with preposition *in*: 'in the loving of ...'

8. ut + subjunctive of late-Latin compound verb *complaceo, complacere* (from *cum* + impersonal verb *placet*) – takes the dative, hence *sibi* (i.e. Jesus): 'in order that I may greatly please him'

9. *istud agas* – neuter *istud* ('that thing') and subjunctive of *ago, agere*

10. *crucifixi* – genitive of *crucifixus*; *fige* – imperative of *figo, figere*, followed by *cordi meo* – dative, so: 'drive the wounds of the crucified through my heart'

11. *valide* – adverb, 'strongly'

12. *tui ... divide* – English word-order is: *divide* (imperative of *divido, dividere*) *mecum* (ablative) *poenas* (accusative plural) *tui vulnerati* (perfect passive participle of *vulnero, vulnerare*) *nati* (genitive), (supply *qui*) *tam dignati* (genitive, because agreeing with *nati*, of *dignatus*, perfect participle of deponent verb *dignor*) *pati* (infinitive of deponent verb *patior*) *pro me* (ablative): 'divide with me the wounds of your wounded son who so deigned to suffer for me'

Fac me vere tecum flere
crucifixo condolere
donec ego vixero.

Iuxta crucem tecum stare,
te libenter sociare,
in planctu desidero.

Virgo virginum praeclara,
mihi iam non sis amara
fac me tecum plangere.

Fac, ut portem Christi mortem,
passionis fac consortem,
et plagas recolere.

Notes for stanzas 13–16:

1. *vere* – adverb, 'truly'

2. *flere* – infinitive of *fleo*, 'weep'

3. condolere – infinitive of *condoleo* takes dative, *crucifixo*: 'feel the pain of the crucifixion'

4. vixero – future perfect tense of *vivo, vivere*, literally: 'I will have lived', i.e. 'while I am alive'

5. iuxta ... desidero – English word-order: *desidero stare tecum iuxta crucem* ...

6. stare – infinitive of *sto, stare*, recalling the very first stanza

7. libenter – adverb, 'willingly'

8. sociare – infinitive of *socio*

9. in + ablative of *planctus*

10. desidero – present tense

11. virgo ... praeclara – noun and adjective, nominative; *virginum* – genitive plural of *virgo, virginis*

12. sis – subjunctive of *sum, esse*; *amara* – feminine of adjective *amarus, -a, -um*: 'may you not be bitter/severe to(wards) me'

13. plangere – infinitive of *plango*, 'grieve'

14. ut + portem – present subjunctive of *porto, portare*: 'that I may carry ...'

15. passionis – genitive; *consortem* – accusative, 'a sharing in'. Supply *me* as in the previous line: 'make me share in his suffering'

16. recolere – infinitive of *recolo*, 'recall, reflect upon' (English 'recollection')

Fac me plagis vulnerari,
cruce hac inebriari
ob amorem Filii

Inflammatus et accensus
per te, Virgo, sim defensus
in die iudicii.

Fac me cruce custodiri,
morte Christi praemuniri,
confoveri gratia.

Quando corpus morietur,
fac ut animae donetur
paradisi gloria.
Amen.

Notes for stanzas 17-20:

1. plagis – ablative plural, 'with his wounds'
2. vulnerari ... inebriari – passive infinitives of *vulnero, vulnerare*: 'to be wounded', and *inebrio, inebriare*: 'to be drunk' so here 'steeped' or 'filled'
3. hac cruce – ablative: the thing the poet wishes to be filled with or steeped in
4. ob + accusative – 'on acount of ...', 'because of ...'
5. Filii – genitive of *Filius*, 'son' in the sense of Father-Son-Holy Ghost rather than birth son of Mary (*natus*)
6. inflammatus ... accensus ... defensus – perfect passive participles of *inflammo, inflammare, accendo, accendere* and *defendo, defendere*: 'inflamed ... set on fire ... defended'
7. per + accusative of *tu*; *virgo* – vocative
8. sim – subjunctive of *sum, esse*: 'may I be ...'
9. in + ablative of *dies* = 'on the ...'; *iudicii* – genitive of *iudicium*
10. custodiri ... praemuniri – passive infinitives of *custodio, custodire*: 'to be guarded', and *praemunio, praemunire*, 'to be fortified'
11. cruce ... morte – ablatives: the things which the poet wishes to be guarded by and fortified with
12. confoveri – passive infinitive of *confoveo, confovere*: 'to be cherished ...'; *gratia* – ablative, '... by His grace'
13. morietur – future tense of deponent verb *morior*
14. animae – dative: 'to my soul'; *donetur* – present passive subjunctive of dono, donare: 'let x be given ...'
15. paradisi – genitive of *paradisum*; *gloria* – nominative: together making the x in 'let x be given to my soul'

Recommended reading:

F.J.E. Raby   *History of Christian-Latin Poetry*
Clarendon Press
First published in 1927, this scholarly work remains the definitive study of sacred Latin.

Recommended listening:

Notable settings of the *Stabat Mater*, all of which are available on CD, include those by:

Palestrina	(1590)
Vivaldi	(1715)
Pergolesi	(1736) Possibly the most sensitive setting of the words
Haydn	(1767)
Rossini	(1837) A florid operatic version
Dvořák	(1877) A monumental work
Stanford	(1906)
Szymanowski	(1926)
Howells	(1965)

There are many others.

CHAPTER 13

CARMINA BURANA & SECULAR LATIN

Secular Latin poetry did not disappear with the passing of pagan Rome and the Christian Church's subsequent monopoly on Latin. Throughout the medieval period and beyond – and despite the growth of vernacular poetry – Latin was still used to write secular verse. Naturally, such worldly Latin was composed by those for whom Latin was the *lingua franca*: the clergy, monks, or students and professors at the new universities.

1. *Carmina Burana: O Fortuna*

The various and mostly anonymous authors responsible for the collection of poems now known as the *Carmina Burana* were a motley assortment of disaffected monks, students and *clerici vagrantes* ('wandering clergy'), often referred to collectively as 'Goliards', an obscure catch-all term for these writers of satirical and/or profane songs about love, sex, drinking, gambling and other vagaries of Fortune.

The manuscript, once housed in the Bavarian monastery of Benediktbeuern, was first published in 1847 under the title *Carmina Burana* ('Songs from Benediktbeuern'). In 1937, German composer and music educationalist Carl Orff (1895-1982) made a selection of the pieces for his music-drama, subtitled:

Cantiones profanae cantoribus et choris cantandae comitantibus instrumentis atque imaginibus magicis

Profane songs for singers and choruses to be sung together with instruments and magic images

Although the original manuscript collection contained *neumes* (see Chapter 10), indicating the Plainchant melodies, Orff chose to compose entirely new music. His setting does, however, hark back to medieval forms by eschewing 'sophisticated' Classical music models,

---

Orff's *Carmina*

Orff selected 25 songs from the Benediktbeuern manuscript – with *O Fortuna* featuring twice at the beginning and end of the work under the heading *Fortuna Imperatrix Mundi* (*Imperatrix* – feminine form of *Imperator*, agreeing with feminine noun *Fortuna*; *Mundi* – genitive of *Mundus*). Inbetween there are three sections headed *Primo Vere*, *In Taberna* and *Cour d'Amour*. Some of the songs mix Latin with vernacular French or German.

---

preferring monophonic choral writing and simple, direct rhythms.

The opening choral *O Fortuna* – an invocation to fickle Fate – is the work's signature piece, and has been used widely in TV ads (e.g. Old Spice aftershave) and movies (e.g. *Excalibur*, *Natural Born Killers*).

O Fortuna,
velut luna
statu variabilis,
semper crescis
aut decrescis;
vita detestabilis
nunc obdurat
et tunc curat
ludo mentis aciem,
egestatem,
potestatem
dissolvit ut glaciem.

Sors immanis
et inanis,
rota tu volubilis,
status malus,
vana salus
semper dissolubilis,
obumbrata
et velata

michi quoque niteris;
nunc per ludum
dorsum nudum
fero tui sceleris.

Sors salutis
et virtutis
michi nunc contraria,
est affectus
et defectus
semper in angaria.
Hac in hora
sine mora
corde pulsum tangite;
quod per sortem
sternit fortem,
mecum omnes plangite!

Notes:

1. O Fortuna – the Latin vocative case does not necessarily require 'O', but the four-syllable metre of the line does
2. statu – ablative of *status*: 'variable in condition/state'
3. crescis ... decrescis – simple present tenses, second person ('you ...') because directly addressing Fortune, of *cresco, crescere* and *decresco, decrescere*
4. obdurat ... curat – subject is *vita* object is *aciem* below
5. ludo mentis aciem – a very difficult line to render literally. The 'detestable life now hardens and then attends to the keeness (*aciem*) of the mind (*mentis*) in/by/with a game (*ludo*)', i.e. life plays a game with us
6. egestatem ... potestatem – both accusative, objects of verb *dissolvit*
7. dissolvit – present tense of *dissolvo, dissolvere*, subject is still *vita*
8. ut glaciem – 'like ice', *glaciem* is accusative, supply *sol* ('the sun') as the subject: life dissolves x and y just as the sun melts ice
9. sors – vocative, 'a lot' as in 'drawing lots', so 'chance', another word for Fortune
10. rota tu volubilis – supply verb *es* with *tu*: 'you are ...' addressing *sors*, also for the next two lines
11. malus ... vana – adjectives agreeing with *status* (masculine) and *salus* (feminine)

12. obumbrata ... velata – adjectives, feminine because agreeing with *sors*

13. michi – Medieval Latin for *mihi*, dative because verb *nitor* takes the dative case

14. niteris – future tense of deponent verb *nitor* (so active not passive)

15. per + accusative of *ludus*, with *tui sceleris* – genitive

16. dorsum nudum – accusative following verb *fero*. English word-order is: *nunc per ludum tui sceleris fero meum nudum dorsum*, 'now through the game of your villainy I bear my naked back'

17. salutis ... virtutis – genitives of *salus* and *virtus*

18. contraria – feminine adjective agreeing with *sors*; takes dative hence *mi(c)hi*

19. est affectus ... in angaria – English word-order: *semper in angaria est affectus et defectus*, 'always in servitude there is both affection and its absence'

20. hac – ablative with *hora*, following preposition *in*

21. mora – ablative of *mos, moris* following preposition *sine*

22. corde – ablative of *cor, cordis*, 'in the heart', with *pulsum*, accusative of *pulsus*

23. tangite – imperative plural of *tango, tangere*

24. quod – 'because'

25. sortem – accusative of *sors*, following preposition *per*

26. sternit fortem – subject of verb *sternit* is *fortuna*; *fortem* – accusative of *fortis*, adjective 'strong/powerful' here used as noun, i.e. 'the strong man'

27. mecum – ablative from pronoun *me* + *cum*, 'with me'

28. plangite – imperative plural of *plango, plangere*

2. *Gaudeamus igitur*

Gaudeamus igitur (also known as *De brevitate vitae*, 'On the shortness of life') apparently dates from the thirteenth century, though the version known today can only be certainly dated from the eighteenth century, by which time it had established itself as a popular student drinking song throughout Europe. It is an example of a *commercium*, a 'commercial song' for a trade or organisation, in this case a university. The climax of Brahms's *Academic Festival Overture* quotes the melody, and the song was famously recorded by Mario Lanza.

The verses below represent the original text as published by Christian Wilhelm Kindleben (1748-1785) in 1781 – there are several variant and often shorter versions.

Gaudeamus igitur,
Iuvenes dum sumus;
Post iucundam iuventutem,
Post molestam senectutem
Nos habebit humus.

Vita nostra brevis est,
Brevi finietur;
Venit mors velociter,
Rapit nos atrociter;
Nemini parcetur.

Ubi sunt, qui ante nos
In mundo fuere?
Vadite ad superos,
Transite ad inferos,
Hos si vis videre.

Vivat academia,
Vivant professores,
Vivat membrum quodlibet,
Vivat membra quaelibet;
Semper sint in flore.

Vivat et respublica
Et qui illam regit,
Vivat nostra civitas,
Maecenatum caritas,
Quae nos hic protegit.

Vivant omnes virgines,
Faciles, formosae,
Vivant et mulieres,
Tenerae, amabiles,
Bonae, laboriosae.

Pereat tristitia,
Pereant osores,
Pereat diabolus
Quivis antiburschius,
Atque irrisores.

Quis confluxus hodie
Academicorum?
E longinquo convenerunt,
Protinusque successerunt
In commune forum.

Vivat nostra societas,
Vivant studiosi!
Crescat una veritas,
Floreat fraternitas,
Patriae prosperitas.

Alma Mater floreat,
Quae nos educavit;
Caros et commilitones,
Dissitas in regiones
Sparsos, congregavit.

Notes:

1. gaudeamus – present subjunctive ('let us ...') of *gaudeo, gaudere*
2. line 2 word-order: *dum sumus iuvenes*, 'while we are young'
3. post + accusative of feminine nouns *iuventus* and *senectus*, and adjectives *iucundus, -a, -um* and *molestus, -a, -um*
4. habebit – future tense of *habeo, habere*, subject is *humus*
5. nostra – adjective agreeing with *vita*
6. brevi – ablative of *brevis*, 'in a brief while'
7. finietur – future passive of *finio, finire*, 'it will be finished'
8. velociter ... atrociter – adverbs, from adjective *velox* and *atrox*
9. mors – subject of verbs *venit ... rapit*, from *venio, venire* and *rapio, rapere*
10. parcetur – future passive of *parco, parcere* + dative (hence *nemini*, from *nemo*)
11. in + ablative of *mundus*

12. fuere – shortened form of *fuerunt*, perfect tense of *sum, esse*; subject is *qui*, nominative plural: 'those who were ...'

13. vadite ... transite – plural imperatives of *vado, vadere* and *transeo, transire*

14. superos ... inferos – accusative plurals (following preposition *ad*) of *superus* and *inferus*, the upper and lower regions respectively

15. hos – accusative plural of pronoun *hic; vis* – second person singular of *volo*

16. videre – infinitive of *video*

17. vivat ... vivant – present subjunctives of *vivo, vivere*

18. membrum ... membra – masculine and feminine 'members' respectively, though noun is neuter, so in proper Classical Latin *membra* is neuter plural not feminine; *quodlibet ... quaelibet* – masculine and feminine adjectives

19. sint – present subjunctive of *sunt*

20. in flore – ablative of *flos, floris*

21. qui – nominative singular, subject of *regit; illam*, accusative referring to *respublica*

22. *Maecenatum* – genitive plural of *Maecenas*, a Roman patron of literature and arts under the Emperor Augustus, metaphorically referring to all patrons

23. quae – relative pronoun referring to *caritas*, nominative because subject of the verb *protegit*

24. hic – 'here'

25. virgines ... mulieres – the contrast is between young maidens and older women

26. faciles, formosae – adjectives agreeing with femininr plural *virgines*

27. mulieres – feminine plural followed by four adjectives describing them

28. pereat ... pereant – present subjunctives of *pereo, perire*, so 'let them perish'

29. osores – plural of *osor*

30. quivis – pronoun, 'whoever'

31. antiburschius – *ante* + a Latinised version of a German word for the student fraternity = 'against the school'

32. irrisores – plural of *irrisor*

33. quis – introducing a question: 'who?'

34. confluxus – perfect passive participle of *confluo, confluere; academicorum* – genitive plural. Literally: 'who having-been-flocked together of the university'

35. longinquo – ablative of *longinquus*

36. convenerunt – perfect of *convenio, convenire*
37. protinus – adverb, 'immediately'
38. successerunt – perfect of *succedo, succedere*
39. commune – adverb, 'communally', 'jointly'; *in* + accusative *forum*
40. studiosi – plural of *studiosus*
41. crescat – present subjunctive of *cresco, crescere*; *una* – adjective agreeing with *veritas*
42. floreat – present subjunctive of *floreo, florere*
43. patriae – genitive
44. alma mater – literally 'nourishing mother' (see Chapter 3)
45. quae – relative pronoun referring to *mater*
46. educavit – perfect tense of *educo, educare*
47. caros – accusative plural of *carus*; *commilitones* – accusative plural of *commilito*
48. dissitas – accusative feminine plural of adjective *dissitus*, agreeing with *regiones*
49. sparsos – perfect participle passive, accusative plural (agreeing with *caros … commilitones*) of *spargo, spargere*
50. congregavit – perfect tense of *congrego, congregare*, subject is still *Alma Mater*

Recommended reading:

J.L. Sebesta   *Carmina Burana*
Bolchazy-Carducci
A line-by-line translation, with vocabulary and notes, of Orff's selection of the *Carmina*.

F.J.E. Raby   *A History of Secular Latin Poetry in the Middle Ages* (2 vols)
Clarendon Press
First published in 1934, Raby's scholarly book predate's Orff's music, but it does include a critical commentary on the Benediktbeuern collection.

CHAPTER 14

ROMAN INSCRIPTIONS

Latin inscriptions of the Roman era survive in their thousands. Some remain *in situ* after more than 2000 years on buildings such as the Pantheon in Rome or on the many triumphal arches across the Empire. More still are found on (mostly) stone fragments in museums around the world, having been unearthed from ruins and in some cases painstakingly reconstructed.

Those written on less durable materials have perished – with a few notable exceptions, such as graffiti and electioneering slogans painted on walls in Pompeii, papyrus fragments preserved in the arid sands of Egypt and the wooden 'notebooks' from Vindolanda on Hadrian's Wall. These sparse examples remind us that although stone inscriptions survive in disproportionate numbers, they were only a small part of 'everyday' Latin in the Roman world.

In this chapter we will look at several examples of real Roman inscriptions. Each example is presented in this format:

- A box with the text reproducing or at least approximating how it appears in the original
- An expanded version of the text, filling out all the abbreviations when applicable
- Grammar and explanatory background notes

SOME COMMONLY USED PHRASES AND ABBREVIATIONS

AVG/AVGG (Augustus/Augusti)
Emperor/Emperors – the number of Gs corresponding to the number of Emperors

COS (Cosol)
Consul – *Cosol* was the ancient spelling

DED (Dedit)
'Gave'. Perfect tense of *do, dare*

DE SP (De Sua Pecunia)

'from his own money', ablative

D M (Dis Manibus)

'to the spirits of the departed', dative plural

D N (Dominus Noster)

'our emperor'

F, FEC (Fecit/Fecerunt)

'(he/they) did'. Perfect tense of *facio, facere*

H F C (Heres Faciendum Curavit/Heredes Faciendum Curaverunt)

'The heir(s) saw to this [monument] being made'. *Faciendum* is the gerundive of *facio, facere*

H S E (Hic Situs/Sita Est)

'here is laid', i.e. 'here lies'. Perfect passive of *sino, sinere* – endings -*us* or -*a* depends on gender

IMP (Imperator, Imperatoris)

Emperor

I O M (Iovi Optimo Maximo)

'To Jupiter, Best and Greatest'. Dative: nominative is *Iuppiter Optimus Maximus*

P P (Pater Patriae)

Father of his country (literally 'of the Fatherland') – an honorary Imperial title

P M (Pontifex Maximus)

Chief Priest – another honorary Imperial title

PR PR (Pro Praetore)

'with the powers of a Praetor', ablative

S C (Senatus Consulto)

'by a decree of the Senate'. *Consulto*, ablative; *Senatus*, genitive

S P Q R (Senatus Populusque Romanus)

'The Senate and People of Rome'

S T T L (Sit Tibi Terra Levis)

'may the earth lie lightly on you'. A traditional funerary formula. *Sit* is subjunctive of *sum, esse*

TR P/TRIB POT (Tribunicia Potestate)

'with tribunician power', ablative. A provincial governor invested with the powers of a Tribune

V S L L M (Votum Solvit Laetus Libens Merito)

'fulfilled his vow gladly, willingly, deservedly'. Translate adjectives *laetus* and *libens* as adverbs

A. FUNERARY INSCRIPTIONS

Gravestones and tombstones are a rich source of surviving Roman inscriptions, as well as an invaluable resource for historians.

Translation tips:

- Often begins *Dis Manibus* (D M) – 'to the spirits of the departed'. *Dis* from *di*, the irregular nominative plural of second declension noun *deus* (also found regularly as *dei*)
- Often ends *hic situs est* (H S E) – 'here lies' or *heres faciendum curavit* (H F C) – 'the heir erected this [monument]'

1. *Extract from an epitaph for a young boy (c.130 B.C., Rome)*

> L. OPTATUS
> VIXIT ANNOS VI MENSES VII ...
> OPTATE SIT TIBI TERRA LEVIS

Expanded text:

Libertus Optatus vixit annos VI menses VIII ... Optate sit tibi terra levis

Notes:

1. Optatus, from the verb *opto, optare*, 'wish' or 'desire', means 'the desired one' – a poignant indication of how precious he was to his parents

2. vixit – perfect tense of *vivo, vivere*

3. Optate – vocative case, addressing the deceased

4. sit – subjunctive of *sum*, here expressing a wish

5. tibi – dative, referring to Optatus

6. terra – nominative

7. levis – adjective agreeing with *terra*. Literally: 'may the earth be light upon you'. More easily translated into English as an adverb, 'lightly'

8. sit tibi terra levis – a traditional formula

9. These words have been set to music by Stephen Hartke as part of a piece entitled *Tituli*, recorded by the Hilliard Ensemble for the ECM label in 2003. The full epitaph text is fragmentary

2. Roman Funerary Marker (Capitoline Museum, Rome)

OSSA
POMPONIAE C L
PLATVRAE

Expanded:

Ossa Pomponiae Caii Libertae Platurae

Notes:

1. This modest plaque was probably intended for a niche in a communal burial vault known as a *columbarium* ('dovecote')

2. ossa – plural of *os, ossis*, 'bone' (English 'ossify'), not to be confused in the nominative/accusative singular with *os, oris*, 'mouth' (English 'oral')

3. Pomponiae ... Platurae – genitive: 'the bones of ...'

4. Caii libertae – also genitive. A freed slave took the name of their former master in this manner (see Chapter 5)

3. Tombstone of Flavia Victorina, Calleva Atrebatum (Silchester)

MEMORIAE
FL VICTORI

```
NAE T TAM
VICTOR
CONIVNX
POSVIT
```

Expanded:

Memoriae Flaviae Victorinae Titus Tammonius Victor Coniunx Posuit

Notes:

1. memoriae – dative, 'to the memory of ...'
2. Flaviae Victorinae – genitive, following *Memoriae*
3. Titus Tammonius Victor – nominative
4. coniunx – nominative, 'spouse', agreeing with *Titus*, so 'husband'
5. posuit – perfect tense of *pono, ponere*

4. Gravestone of Caecilius Avitus, Deva (Chester)

```
D M
CAECILIVS AVIT
VS EMER AUG
OPTIO LEG XX
V V STP XV VIX
AN XXXIIII
H F C
```

Expanded:

Dis Manibus Caecilius Avitus Emerita Augusta Optio Legionis XX Valeriae Victricis Stipendiorum XV Vixit Annos XXXIIII Heres Faciendum Curavit

Notes:

1. Dis Manibus – the traditional invocation in the dative case to the departed spirits
2. Caecilius Avitus – the name of the deceased in the nominative case, not the genitive (which would make the phrase 'to the departed spirits of ...')
3. Emerita Augusta – his home town, now Merida in Spain. Ablative case

4. Optio – his rank, the second-in-command of a century
5. Legionis XX – genitive case, 'of the Twentieth legion'
6. Valeriae Victricis – genitive, agreeing with *legionis*: 'Valeria Victorious'. The exact meaning of *Valeria* is obscure, it may be an adjective derived from the verb *valeo, valere*, meaning 'valiant'
7. stipendiorum XV – genitive plural of *stipendium*, the term for military service (English 'stipend')
8. vixit – perfect tense of *vivo, vivere*
9. annos – accusative plural
10. heres faciendum curavit – a traditional formula. The verb *curo* plus the gerundive = 'to see to a thing being done'

B. ALTARS

Romans dedicated altars to the gods for many reasons but primarily as a thanks-offering for help received. Roman religion took the form of a business contract between gods and worshippers – the worshipper asked for a favour to be granted and if the gods fulfilled their part of the bargain, they were rewarded with an altar such as those below.

Translation tips:

- Often begins with the name of the god/goddess being venerated in the dative case, followed by the name of the dedicatee in the nominative
- Often ends with the formula *votum solvit laetus libens merito* (V S L L M) – 'fulfilled his vow gladly, willingly, deservedly'

1. *Mithraic Altar from Vindobala (Rudchester, Hadrian's Wall)*

The mystery cult of Mithras, which originated in the East, became increasingly popular throughout the Roman Empire, as the number of Mithraic temples and altars attest. Mithras, a divinity of light and the sun, promised salvation to those who had been initiated into his rites and undergone certain trials. The cult was popular among soldiers and attracted adherents from many social backgrounds, including slaves, but like modern Freemasonry it excluded women.

DEO INVICTO
MYTRAE P AEL
FLAVINVS PRAE
V S L L M

Expanded:

Deo Invicto Mytrae Publius Aelius Flavinus Praefectus Votum Solvit Laetus Libens Merito

Notes:

1. Deo Invicto Mytrae – dative case, the traditional formula invoking the god, despite the idiosyncratic spelling, traditionally referred to as 'invincible' or 'unconquered'
2. Publius ... praefectus – all nominative, the person dedicating the altar
3. V S L L M – the traditional formula

2. *Mithraic Altar from Brocolitia (Carrawburgh, Hadrian's Wall)*

D IN M S
AV CLVENTIVS
HABITVS PRAF
COH I BATAVORVM
DOMV VLTI
NA COLON
SEPT AVR L
V S L M

Expanded:

Deo Invicto Mithrae Sacrum Aulus Cluentius Habitus Praefectus Cohortis I Batavorum Domu Ultinia Colonia Septimia Aurelia Larino Votum Solvit Libens Merito

Notes:

1. Deo Invicto Mithrae – dative
2. sacrum – 'Sacred to ...'
3. Aulus Cluentius Habitus – nominative. Almost certainly one

of the *Cluentii* from the town of Larinum made famous in one of Cicero's most brilliant speeches, *Pro Cluentio*, 'In defence of Cluentius', in which he defended another relative of the same name on a charge of murder

4.　Cohortis ... Batavorum – genitive

5.　domu – ablative, literally 'home' but here referring to the voting tribe, more usually *tribus*, 'tribe', ablative *tribu*

6.　Ultinia – variant spelling of *Voltinia*, one of the 35 ancient Roman voting tribes. The practice of adding the voting tribe on monuments began to be abandoned by the second century A.D., as the whole idea of voting was an empty formality by then

7.　Colonia Septimia Aurelia Larino – ablative, 'from the town ...'

8.　V S L M – the traditional formula, only lacking *laetus*

3. *Altar from Verocovicium (Housesteads on Hadrian's Wall)*

An example of the inclusive nature of Roman religion:

```
        I O M
   ET DEO COCIDIO
    GENIOQ HVIS
    LOCI MIL LEG
   II AVG AGENTES
    IN PRAESIDIO
       V S L M
```

Expanded:

Iovi Optimo Maximo et Deo Cocidio Genioque Huius Loci Milites Legionis II Augustae Agentes In Praesidio Votum Solverunt Libentes Merito

Notes:

1.　I O M – dative, addressing Jupiter with his traditional epithets 'best and greatest'

2.　Deo Cocidio – dative. Cocidius was a native British deity, equated by the Roman soldiers with both the Latin hunting god Silvanus and Mars, god of war. It was characteristic of Roman religion to absorb native rites in this manner. A portrait of Cocidius also from Hadrian's Wall survives showing him as a horned god carrying a spear and shield

3. genio ... loci – the *Genius* of the place, the spirit that dwelt there
    and provided protection. Each Roman household also had a
    Genius, symbolised by a snake, as did every man – the indwelling
    spirit that gave him fertility (the corresponding female spirit was
    a *Iuno*)
4. huius – genitive, 'of this place'
5. milites – nominative plural, they are all dedicating this altar
6. Legionis II Augustae – genitive
7. agentes in praesidio – *agentes*, present participle of *ago, agere*,
    literally: 'those engaged upon [duty] in the garrison'
8. solverunt ... libentes – plural, because *milites* is plural

C. MONUMENTAL INSCRIPTIONS

Inscriptions on public buildings typically dedicate them to the
reigning Emperor as well as recording the person or group (army
unit, city authority etc.) who either paid for or erected the building.
Only rarely does the text name the actual building – that would be
redundant when the plaque would originally have been attached.
Inscriptions on statue bases record the deeds of the person whose
image stands on the plinth.

Translation tip:

•   The name(s) of the Emperor(s) are often given in the dative
    case, since the inscription is a dedication *to* them. Also look
    out for the word *fecit* (singular) or *fecerunt* (plural) – 'built it'

1. *The Pantheon, Rome*

One of the most wondrous buildings in Rome, if not in the world,
the Pantheon remains remarkably intact after 2000 years. Its concrete
dome roof was the largest in the world until the building of St.
Peter's across the river in the Vatican. On the front pediment a simple
inscription reads:

M. AGRIPPA L F COS TERTIVM FECIT

Expanded:

Marcus Agrippa Lucii Filius Consul Tertium Fecit

Notes:

1. M Agrippa L F – *praenomen* (abbreviated to M) *cognomen* (both in the nominative case) *nomen* (genitive case) *filius* (nominative): 'Marcus Agrippa, son of Lucius'. His full name is *Marcus Lucius Agrippa* (see Chapter 5 for Roman names)
2. cos – derives from the old Roman spelling of *consul*, which once was *cosol*
3. tertium – 'three times'
4. fecit – perfect tense of *facio, facere*, 'to make, do'. In this context 'built'

2. *The Arch of Titus, Rome*

> SENATVS
> POPVLVSQVE ROMANVS
> DIVO TITO DIVI VESPASIANI F
> VESPASIANO AVGVSTO

Expanded:

Senatus Populusque Romanus Divo Tito Divi Vespasiani Filio Vespasiano Augusto

Notes:

1. Senatus Populusque Romanus – SPQR – the famous Roman formula, carried everywhere on legionary standards and still to be seen even on manhole covers in Roman streets!
2. Tito ...Vespasiano – the name of the dedicatee in the dative case: 'to Titus Vespasian'
3. divo ... Augusto – also in the dative case, agreeing with the name: 'to the deified ...Augustus'
4. filio – also dative, in agreement with *Tito Vespasiano*
5. divi Vespasiani – genitive case, 'son of the deified Vespasian'
6. both father and son have been deified, so this inscription dates from after the son's death in A.D. 81

3. Slab from Bremenium (High Rochester)

From a fort north of Hadrian's Wall on Dere Street, *circa* third century A.D.

> VEXILLATO
> LEG XX V V
> FECIT

Expanded:
Vexillato Legionis XX Valeriae Victricis Fecit

Notes:
1. vexillato – a detachment of legionary troops on special duty
2. legionis – genitive
3. Valeriae Victricis – genitive, agreeing with *legionis*. The name *Valeria Victrix* may have been given to the legion for their part in suppressing the revolt of Boudicca in A.D. 61
4. fecit – perfect tense of *facio, facere*

4. Verulamium (St Albans)

> IMP TITO CAESARI DIVI VESPASIANI F VESPASIANO AVG
> PM TRP VIIII IMP XV COS VII DESIG VIII CENSORI
> PATRI PATRIAE
> ET CAESARI DIVI VESPASIANI F DOMITIANO COS VI
> DESIG VII PRINCIPI
> IVVENTVTIS ET OMNIVM COLLEGIORVM SACERDOTI
> CN IVLIO AGRICOLA LEGATO AVG PRO PR
> MUNICIPIVM VERVLAMIVM BASILICA ORNATA

Expanded:
Imperatori Tito Caesari Divi Vespasiani Filio Vespasiano Augusto Pontifici Maximo Tribuniciae Potestate VIIII Imperatori XV Consuli VII Designato VIII Censori Patri Patriae et Caesari Divi Vespasiani Filio Domitiano Consuli VI Designato VII Principi Iuventutis et Omnium Collegiorum

Sacerdoti Cnaeo Iulio Agricola Legato Augusti Pro Praetore Municipium Verulamium Basilica Ornata

Notes:

1. This inscription is a reconstruction based on fragments discovered in 1955. The full-size recreation of the stone can be seen in the Verulamium Museum, though the reading of *Municipium Verulamium* in the last line is possibly erroneous

2. imperatori Tito Caesari Vespasiano Aug – all dative, addressing. Titus was Augustus from A.D. 79-81, and held his seventh consulship in 79, thus providing a solid date

3. designato – dative of *designatus*, 'designated' i.e. already chosen as consul for the following year

4. Caesari Domitiano – dative, note Domitian not addressed as Augustus, he was still just the junior rank of 'Caesar'

5. principi ... sacerdoti – both dative, agreeing with *Domitiano*

6. Cnaeo Iulio Agricola Legato – ablative of time, just as with the expression *Cicerone consule*, 'in the consulship of Cicero': here 'while Agricola was legate'. Agricola was the father-in-law of the historian Tacitus, who wrote a biography of him in which he describes Agricola's encouragement of public building projects in Britain. This inscription provides solid proof of Tactitus' remarks

7. ornata – perfect passive participle of *orno, ornare*, agreeing with *basilica* – I read it as an ablative absolute construction, i.e. 'The municipium of Verulamium in the praetorship of Agricola, *having furnished this basilica*, [dedicate it] to the Emperor Titus Vespasian ...'

Recommended reading:

J. Rogan   *Reading Roman Inscriptions*
                 Tempus Publishing
An excellent 'how to' guide that provides all the rules and formulae
necessary for understanding Roman inscriptions.

L. Keppie   *Understanding Roman Inscriptions*
                 Routledge
A good introduction to the subject for the general reader, with lots
of historical background.

Dobson & Maxfield (eds)   *Inscriptions of Roman Britain:*
                             Lactor 4
                             London Association of Classical
                             Teachers
A handy paperback compendium of Romano-British inscriptions
with translations.

CHAPTER 15

LATIN EPITAPHS

Throughout Britain epitaphs on tombstones and funerary monuments were frequently written in Latin, especially from the sixteenth to nineteenth centuries, a period when Classical learning was most highly prized. Dr Johnson summed up the prevailing view of the times when he said, 'The language of the country, of which a learned man

Epitaph

English 'epitaph' derives from the French *epitaphe*, from the Latin *epitaphium*, which itself is just a Latinised version of the Greek επιταφιον, originally an adjectival description of a funeral oration, then applied to the words inscribed on the tomb itself. The word first appears in English in the fourteenth century.

was a native, is not the language fit for his epitaph, which should be in ancient and permanent language' (*Life of Johnson*). Latin seemed more fitting to be carved in stone than the current vernacular – hundreds of years later our own language may have changed almost beyond recognition, but Latin will endure unaltered. (Though the ability to read it assumed that Latin would remain part of the school curriculum!)

As a result, cathedrals and churches across Britain, not to mention throughout Europe, are full of stone monuments commemorating local families and dignitaries in more-or-less correct Latin. Some can be challenging to read for various reasons: either they are badly worn by weather, or the lettering has faded over time; or, indeed, they contain spelling and grammatical errors that need to be identified and corrected by the would-be translator. Consider that most stonemasons who carved the inscriptions did not understand Latin, that they were working from handwritten perhaps partly illegible texts, and that once a mistake is made on stone it's difficult if not impossible to correct, then it's hardly surprising that such errors should have arisen quite frequently.

Nevertheless, despite the challenges of translating, one of the most rewarding aspects of learning 'everyday Latin' is being able to impress your friends by reading these memorials in churches and cathedrals across the country!

In this chapter we will look at some typical examples, using the same basic layout as the Roman inscriptions in Chapter 14. As with those texts, it is necessary to understand the shorthand that the writers often employed in order to save space on the stone. So first of all, some tips:

Translation tips:

- As well as the familiar ampersand (&) being used in place of the Latin *et*, epitaphs often abbreviate *-que* ('and') at the end of a word to *q*.
- Other words where the sense is deemed to be obvious are also contracted, e.g. *Nat.* for *Natus* (*est*), 'born', *Mort.* for *Mortuus* (*est*), 'died', or *In Com.* for *In Comitatu* 'in the County of'
- Look out for commonly recurring key words such as *vixit*, 'lived' and *obiit*, 'died', as well as family relationships such as *uxor*, 'wife', *coniunx*, 'spouse', *frater, soror, mater, pater, filius, filia*. etc.
- Sometimes an accent is placed over letters to indicate a long vowel, when a word looks the same in the ablative singular as it does in the nominative, e.g. *familiâ* (ablative) rather than *familia* (nominative)
- The third person perfect indicative tense ending *-erunt* can be contracted to *-ere*, e.g. *amavere* instead of *amaverunt*
- Medieval Latin spellings are the norm, so j instead of consonantal-i, e.g. *jacet* instead of *iacet*, 'lies'; *ejus* instead of *eius*, 'his'
- Watch out for non-Classical words such as *Armiger* ('Esquire') or Classical words used in a new context, e.g. *Miles* (not 'soldier' but 'Knight')
- English names often have arbitrary Latin declension endings added, e.g. *Natus est Cottinghamiae*, 'he was born at Cottingham'
- Places are sometimes given in an adjectival form, usually identified by some form of the suffix *-ensis*, e.g. *Westmonasteriens*

for 'Westminster' but adjectivally *in schola Westmonastriensi*, 'at Westminster School'

SOME COMMONLY USED PHRASES AND ABBREVIATIONS:

A.C. (Anno Christi)

'in the year of Christ'. A variant on the more common *A.D.*

A.D. (Anno Domini)

'in the year of (our) Lord'. *Anno*, ablative; *Domini*, genitive

A.S. (Anno Salutis)

'in the year of (our) Salvation'. Another variant on *A.D.*

ae. aet. aetat. (aetatis)

'aged'. Literally 'of age' – genitive singular of *aetas*

anno aetatis suae

'in the year of his/her age'. *Anno,* ablative, *suae* adjective agreeing with genitive *aetatis*

c. (circa/circum)

'round about'. Preposition + accusative, usually used with dates

D.D.D. (dono dedit dedicavit)

'gave (and) dedicated as a gift'. *Dono*, dative; *dedit*, perfect tense of *do, dare*; *dedicavit*, perfect tense of of *dedico, dedicare*

D.N.I.C. (Dominus noster Iesus Christus)

'Our Lord Jesus Christ'. All nominative

H.M. (hoc monumentum)

'this monument'. Nominative

H.M.P. (hoc monumentum posuit)

'placed this monument'. *Posuit/posuerunt*, perfect tense of *pono, ponere*. But if *H.M.P.* is followed by *curavit/curaverunt*, then the *P.* is either *poni* or *ponendum* – see *P.C.* below

H.S.E. (hic sepultus/sepulta est)

'here is buried'. Perfect passive of *sepelio, sepelire,* 'bury'. *-us/-a* depends on gender

H.S.E. (hic situs/sita est)

'here is laid'. Perfect passive of *sino, sinere*

hic jacet/iacet

'here lies'

I.H.S. (Iesu Hominum Salvator)

'Jesus Saviour of Men'. *Hominum,* genitive plural of *homo*

in aeternum

'forever'

in memoriam

'in memory (of)'

in perpetuum

'forever'

M.S. (memoriae sacrum)

'sacred to the memory of'. *Memoriae,* dative. Also *S.M.*

ob. (obiit)

'he/she died'. Literally: 'went to meet (death)'

P.C. (poni/ponendum curavit)

'caused to be placed'. *Poni* is the passive infinitive of *pono, ponere.* Alternatively, it could be *ponendum,* the gerundive, but the meaning is the same. *Curo, curare* = 'takes the trouble to ...'

P.M. (piae memoriae)

'to the pious memory of'. Both dative, *piae* is the adjective

R.I.P. (requiescat in pace)

'may he/she rest in peace'. *Requiescat* is the present subjunctive of *requiesco, requiescere*

S.M. (memoriae sacrum)

'sacred to the memory'. *Memoriae* = dative. Also *M.S.*

A. FAMOUS LATIN EPITAPHS

Some examples of epitaphs commemorating some famous names.

1. Samuel Johnson, Poets' Corner, Westminster Abbey

A literary giant of his day, Johnson (1709-84) is remembered by posterity principally in the pages of Boswell's biography, *The Life of Johnson*, still arguably the finest work of its kind. But Johnson wrote prolifically in many genres: essays, periodicals, poetry, novels and wrote the first authoritative *Dictionary of the English Language*. He also wrote much in Latin – poems, prayers and epitaphs – even composing extempore Latin verses when the fancy took him.

This marker, a small flagstone in the floor, is placed directly over Johnson's remains, which lie next to those of his great friend the actor David Garrick. A more florid monument to 'the Great Cham of Literature' is to be found in St Paul's Cathedral.

> SAMUEL JOHNSON, LL.D.
> Obiit XIII die Decembris
> Anno Domini
> M. DCC. LXXXIV.
> Aetatis suae LXXV

Notes:

1. LL.D. – *Legum Doctor*, 'Doctor of Laws' (see Chapter 4: Academic Abbreviations)
2. Obiit – strictly speaking shorthand for the phrase *mortem obiit*, 'met death'
3. die – ablative of *dies*, 'day', so 'on the thirteenth day ...'
4. Decembris – genitive
5. Anno Domini – see abbreviations list above
6. M. DCC. LXXXIV – see Chapter 5 for Roman numerals. Note the unusual spacing
7. Aetatis suae – genitive, 'of his age'

2. *Jonathan Swift, St Patrick's Cathedral, Dublin*

Dean Swift (1667-1745) was perhaps the English language's greatest satirist. In essays, pamphlets and poems he wrote pointedly, humorously and bitterly against injustice and inequality. His most enduring work is of course *Gulliver's Travels*, often thought of as a children's book, but in fact a wide-ranging satire on British political and social institutions.

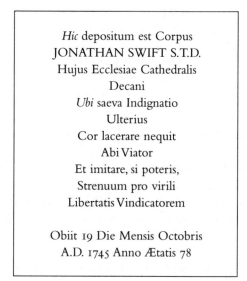

Hic depositum est Corpus
JONATHAN SWIFT S.T.D.
Hujus Ecclesiae Cathedralis
Decani
Ubi saeva Indignatio
Ulterius
Cor lacerare nequit
Abi Viator
Et imitare, si poteris,
Strenuum pro virili
Libertatis Vindicatorem

Obiit 19 Die Mensis Octobris
A.D. 1745 Anno Ætatis 78

Notes:
1. Swift wrote this epitaph himself
2. depositum est – perfect passive of *depono, deponere*, 'lay down'
3. S.T.D. – 'Doctor of Sacrosanct Theology'
4. Hujus Ecclesiae Cathedralis – all genitive: *cathedral* from *cathedra*, the bishop's chair
5. Decani – genitive, because the first line is 'the body of ...'
6. indignatio – nominative: verbs are *lacerare* (infinitive of *lacero*) and *nequit* (from *nequeo*), accusative is *cor*
7. ulterius – adverb, 'any more'
8. abi – imperative of *abeo, abire*, 'go away'
9. imitare – imperative of deponent verb *imitor, imitari*, 'imitate'
10. poteris – future tense of *possum, posse*, 'can'

11. strenuum ... vindicatorem – accusative, the subject is the *Viator*, being exhorted to imitate Dean Swift's example. The word order – adjective at the beginning, noun at the end of the sentence – is intended to emphasise the phrase

12. pro virili – prepositional phrase, 'to the best of one's ability'

13. die – ablative, 'on the nineteenth day'

14. mensis Octobris – genitive, 'of October'

15. William Butler Yeats' poetical paraphrase:

> Swift has sailed into his rest.
> Savage indignation there
> cannot lacerate his breast.
> Imitate him if you can,
> world-besotted traveller.
> He served human liberty.

3. *Oliver Goldsmith, Poets' Corner, Westminster Abbey*

Poet, dramatist and essayist, Goldsmith (1728-74) sadly never found the financial security to match his literary fame and was dogged by illness and poverty throughout much of his life. Among his best known works, still widely read today, are the poem *The Deserted Village*, the comic play *She Stoops to Conquer* and the novel *The Vicar of Wakefield*.

This epitaph was written by Dr Johnson against the advice of his friends, who wanted Goldsmith's memorial to be in English, so records Boswell in his *Life of Johnson*. Johnson, a staunch Latinist, remained unmoved, declaring 'he would never consent to disgrace the walls of Westminster Abbey with an English inscription'. The praise of the epitaph is a little at odds with Johnson's own opinion of some of Goldsmith's literary endeavours. Although he esteemed Goldsmith highly as a writer, it was a bit of a stretch to say that his achievements in natural history equalled his poetry: 'Goldsmith, Sir, will give us a very fine book upon the subject; but if he can distinguish a cow from a horse, that, I believe, may be the extent of his knowledge.' Elsewhere he remarked pithily, 'In lapidary inscriptions a man is not under oath'.

OLIVARII GOLDSMITH,
POETAE, PHYSICI, HISTORICI,
QUI NULLUM FERE SCRIBENDI GENUS
NON TETIGIT,
NULLUM QUOD TETIGIT NON ORNAVIT:
SIVE RISUS ESSENT MOVENDI
SIVE LACRYMAE,
AFFECTUUM POTENS ET LENIS DOMINATOR:
INGENIO SUBLIMIS, VIVIDUS, VERSATILIS,
ORATIONE GRANDIS, NITIDUS, VENUSTUS:
HOC MONUMENTO MEMORIAM COLUIT
SODALIUM AMOR,
AMICORUM FIDES,
LECTORUM VENERATIO.
NATUS IN HIBERNIA FORNIA LONGOFORDIENSIS,
IN LOCO CUI NOMEN PALLAS,
NOV. XXIX. MDCCXXXI;
EBLANAE LITERIS INSTITUTUS:
OBIIT LONDINII,
APRIL IV, MDCCLXXIV

Notes:

1. Olivarii – genitive of *olivarius*. The following epithets are also in the same case: *poetae, physici, historici*. We have to wait until line 11 to find out why

2. qui – now beginning a new clause

3. fere – adverb, 'scarcely', 'hardly'

4. scribendi genus – 'of the writing kind'. *Scribendi* is genitive gerund of *scribo, scribere*

5. tetigit – perfect tense of *tango, tangere*, 'touch' (English 'tangible)

6. ornavit – perfect tense of *orno, ornare*, 'adorn' (English 'ornate')

7. risus ... lachrymae – nominative plurals

8. essent – imperfect subjunctive of *sum, esse*

9. movendi – nominative plural gerundive of *moveo, movere*, agreeing with *risus* and *lacrymae* (variant spelling of *lacrimae*)

10. affectuum – genitive plural

11. dominator – 'absolute ruler', 'despot', derived from the verb

dominor. *Dominus* is the traditional word for 'Master' but presumably Johnson wanted something stronger

12. ingenio ... oratione – ablatives. *Ingenium*, 'character', 'natural ability', 'talent'; *oratio*, 'speech', 'style of language'

13. venustus – 'charming', 'elegant', a word often used by the Roman poet Catullus

14. hoc monumento – ablative

15. coluit – perfect tense of *colo, coluere*, 'cultivate', 'take care of'. Now the reason for Goldsmith's name being in the genitive becomes clear: this monument 'honours the memory of ...'

16. amor ... fides ... veneratio – nominatives: English word-order puts these at the very beginning of the epitaph, though the Latin has them at the end

17. sodalium ... amicorum ... lectorum – genitive plurals

18. natus – for *natus est*, 'he was born'

19. Fornia Longofordiensis – literally 'the Longford Forney'

20. cui nomen Pallas – dative *cui*, understand *est*: 'has the name Pallas'

21. MDCCXXXI – a mistake, he was actually born in 1728

22. Eblanae – locative case: 'at Dublin'

23. literis – ablative plural, 'in letters', variant spelling of *litteris*

24. institutus – literally: 'having been educated'. Perfect passive participle of *instituo, instituere*. He attended Trinity College

25. Londinii – another locative: 'at London'

4. *Sir Christopher Wren, St Paul's Cathedral*

Sir Christopher Wren (1632-1723) was noted in his day as a scientist (he was a Professor of Astronomy as well as a distinguished mathematician), but it is his achievements in architecture that have ensured his permanent fame. The Sheldonian Theatre in Oxford, the Greenwich Naval Hospital, and numerous other buildings and churches attest to Wren's genius, but St Paul's Cathedral is his *magnum opus*.

This epitaph was written by Wren's son. The final epigram is frequently quoted.

SUBTUS CONDITUR
HUIUS ECCLESIAE ET VRBIS CONDITOR
CHRISTOPHORUS WREN
QUI VIXIT ANNOS ULTRA NONAGINTA
NON SIBI SED BONO PUBLICO
LECTOR, SI MONUMENTUM REQUIRIS
CIRCUMSPICE

Obiit XXV Feb An° MDCCXXIII Aet XCI

Notes:

1. conditur – present passive of *condo, condere*, 'bury' in this context
2. huius ecclesiae ... urbis – genitives
3. conditor – a nice play on words, using *condo, condere* again, but in its other sense of 'build' or 'found'. Hence the Roman phrase *Anno Urbis Conditae*, 'in the year of the founding of the city' (see Chapter 5). The suffix *–tor* indicates the person (Doctor, Actor etc.)
4. qui – nominative
5. vixit – perfect tense of *vivo, vivere*
6. annos – accusative
7. ultra – 'beyond' but taken with the accusative means 'more than ...'
8. sibi ... bono publico – dative, not ablative as in the legal phrase *pro bono publico*
9. Lector – vocative, addressing the reader
10. circumspice – imperative, from *circumspicio, circumspicere*: 'Reader, if you seek his monument, look around!'

B. LOCAL LATIN EPITAPHS

Epitaphs like those below are found in many cathedrals and older churches across Britain. Those below just happen to be from churches in my own neighbourhood, but they are representative of this centuries-old tradition, now sadly fallen into abeyance.

1. *St Mary's Church, Amersham, Buckinghamshire*

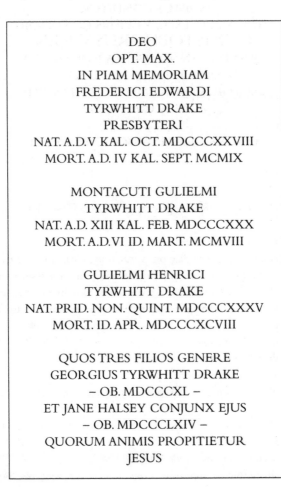

DEO
OPT. MAX.
IN PIAM MEMORIAM
FREDERICI EDWARDI
TYRWHITT DRAKE
PRESBYTERI
NAT. A.D.V KAL. OCT. MDCCCXXVIII
MORT. A.D. IV KAL. SEPT. MCMIX

MONTACUTI GULIELMI
TYRWHITT DRAKE
NAT. A.D. XIII KAL. FEB. MDCCCXXX
MORT. A.D.VI ID. MART. MCMVIII

GULIELMI HENRICI
TYRWHITT DRAKE
NAT. PRID. NON. QUINT. MDCCCXXXV
MORT. ID. APR. MDCCCXCVIII

QUOS TRES FILIOS GENERE
GEORGIUS TYRWHITT DRAKE
– OB. MDCCCXL –
ET JANE HALSEY CONJUNX EJUS
– OB. MDCCCLXIV –
QUORUM ANIMIS PROPITIETUR
JESUS

Notes:

1. Deo Opt. Max. – abbreviation of *Deo Optimo Maximo*, dative case. A Christian variant on the traditional Roman *Iuppiter Optimus Maximus*. The writer of this inscription is keen to demonstrate their Classical credentials, as we will also see with the dates

2. in piam memoriam – 'in pious memory of ...' hence the three names all appear in the genitive case

3. nat a.d. – *natus (est) ante diem* ... See Chapter 5 for Roman dates. Another Classical touch

4. quint – for *Quintilis*, the old Roman name for July, originally the fifth month

5. mort – for *mortuus (est)*, note that *obiit* is used as an alternative below

6. quos tres filios – accusative, the parents named below are the subjects of the verb

7. genere – shortened version of *generaverunt*, perfect tense of the verb *genero, generare*, 'beget'

8. ob. – for *obiit* (properly *mortem obiit*, literally 'met death')

9. quorum – genitive plural, referring to the three sons

10. animis – dative plural

11. The sense of the last line is 'May Jesus have mercy on their souls'. The verb *propitietur* (English 'propitiate') is passive subjunctive (of *propitio, propitiare*). A similar sentiment occurs in the Vulgate's *propitietur vobis, Dominus* (Leviticus, 23/28), which is translated in the King James version as: 'to make an atonement for you before the Lord your God.' Literally the epitaph phrase means 'May Jesus be appeased by their souls', which doesn't sound an especially Christian sentiment – though a Roman would doubtless see nothing wrong with the need to appease (propitiate) a god. Inspired by the King James translation, the verb could be taken as impersonal with the agent (*animis*) in the dative: 'may their souls make an atonement before Jesus'.

2. Edmund Waller, St Mary's Churchyard, Beaconsfield, Buckinghamshire

Edmund Waller (1606-1687) was celebrated in his lifetime as a poet of great distinction and his works influenced his successors, notably Dryden and Pope.

He was a wealthy man from an influential family and was closely involved in the troubled politics of Civil War-torn England, first as a Parliamentarian, then as a staunch Royalist. He spent the years of Cromwell's rule in exile, but returned with the Restoration.

He married twice, though both wives predeceased him. Of his prodigious poetical output, nowadays only *Go, Lovely Rose* is well remembered.

The monument in the churchyard was set up, as the inscription tells us, according to the will of his son Edmund Jr.

Go, lovely Rose

Go, lovely Rose –
Tell her that wastes her time and me,
That now she knows,
When I resemble her to thee,
How sweet and fair she seems to be.

Tell her that's young,
And shuns to have her graces spied,
That hadst thou sprung
In deserts where no men abide,
Thou must have uncommended
    died.

Small is the worth
Of beauty from the light retired:
Bid her come forth,
Suffer herself to be desired,
And not blush so to be admired.

Then die – that she
The common fate of all things rare
May read in thee;
How small a part of time they share
That are so wondrous sweet and
    fair!

On each of the four sides are plaques with the Latin text written by Thomas Rymer, a minor poet of the late seventeenth century.

Heus! Viator, tumulatum vides EDMUNDUM WALLER;
Qui tanti nominis poeta; et idem avitis opibus,
Inter primos, spectabilis; musis se dedit et patriae.
Nondum Octodecinaris, inter ardua regni tractantes
Sedem habuit a Burgo de Amersham missus
Hic vitae cursus: nec onori defuit senex, vixitque semper
Populo charus, Principibus in deliciis, admirationi Omnibus

Hic conditur tumulo sub eodem
Rarâ virtute et multâ prole nobilis
Vxor, MARIA, ex Bressyorum Familiâ
Cum EDMUNDO WALLER conjuge charissimo
Quem ter et decies laetum fecit patrem
V. Filiis et Filiabus VIII.
Quos mundo dedit, et in caelum rediit

Notes:
    1.   viator – vocative

2. tumulatum – perfect passive participle of *tumulo, tumulare*, 'bury', accusative agreeing with *Edmundum*: literally 'Edmund Waller having-been-buried'

3. qui tanti ... opibus – 'he who [was] a Poet of such great name and yet also with ancestral wealth'. Possible implication is that it's unusual to be both? Alternatively ignore the punctuation and take the word order as: *Qui tanti nominis Poeta et idem spectabilis inter primos avitis opibus*

4. se dedit – reflexive: 'he dedicated himself to ...'

5. octodecinaris – in his eighteenth year – ablative plural of *octodecimarius*. *duodeviginti* is more usual for eighteen, *duodevicesimus* = eighteenth

6. tractantes – present participle of the verb *traho*, 'drag', here meaning 'drawn out', 'prolonged' – reading *tractantis*, genitive, in agreement with *regni*

7. sedem habuit – i.e. a seat in Parliament

8. burgo – from burgus, 'fort', whence English '-burgh', '-borough' and 'Bury'

9. de Amersham – here *de* is used instead of the genitive case, as in Romance languages *de/di*, 'of'

10. vitae cursus – cf. *curriculum vitae*

11. onori – either a misspelling of *oneri* (*onus* = 'burden'), or of *honori* (*honos* = 'dignity', 'respect'); verb *defuit* (*desum*) takes the dative

12. charus – misspelling of *carus*

13. principibus – dative, literally 'leaders', 'foremost men', but Waller was a Royalist, so perhaps 'Princes' is better in context?

14. in deliciis – ablative, a set phrase, 'a favourite among ...'

15. admirationi – ablative of *admiratio*

16. tumulo sub eodem – ablative of *tumulus*, echoing *tumulatum* in the first line

17. rara ... multa ... familia – note accents on final *a* to indicate ablative case

18. Bressyorum – a made-up genitive plural: 'of the Bressys'

19. cum + ablative case = 'with ...'

20. charissimo – misspelling of superlative, ablative, *carissimo*

21. ter et decies, literally 'three times and ten times'. *terdecies* more usual for thirteenth

22. Filiis ... Filiabus – to distinguish genders, the third declension ending is used for the first declension noun *filia*, q.v. feminine *dea*, ablative *deabus*, to distinguish from masculine *deus/deis* (or *dis*)

EDMUNDI WALLER hic jacet id quantrum morti cessit
Qui inter poetas sui temporis facile princeps
Lauream quam meruit Adolescens
Octogenarius haud abdicavit
Huic debet patria lingua, quod credas,
Si Graece Latineque intermitterent musae
Loqui, amarent Anglice

Notes:

1. Edmundi – genitive
2. quantrum – misspelling of *quantum*, agrees with *id*
3. morti – dative; *cessit* – perfect of *cedo, cedere*
4. lauream – the laurel crown is the symbol of poets, hence Poet Laureate
5. huic – dative of *hic*; nominative is *patria lingua*
6. quod credas – *quod* + subjunctive (of *credo*), a Medieval Latin construction (= *ut* + subjunctive in Classical Latin): 'you may believe/accept as true'
7. Graece ... Latine ... Anglice – adverbs, 'in the Greek language' etc.
8. intermitterent ... amarent – imperfect subjunctives; the *musae* are the subjects
9. loqui – infinitive of deponent verb *loquor*

EDMUNDUS WALLER, cui hoc marmor sacrum est
Colshill nascendi locum habuit, Cantabrigiam studendi
Patrem ROBERTUM et ex HAMPDENA stirpe matrem;
Coepit vivere 3° Martii A.D. 1605
Prima uxor ANNA EDWARDI BANKS Filia unica et Haeres
Ex prima bis pater factus; ex secunda tredecies
Cui et duo lustra superstes; obiit 21 Octob. A.D. 1687

Notes:

1. nascendi ... studendi – gerunds, genitive of *nascor* and *studeo* with *locum*: 'place of birth/study'
2. habuit – applies to lines 2 & 3

3. haeres – variant spelling of *heres*
4. factus – sc. *est*, 'he was made', subject is still *Edmundus* from line 1
5. tredecies – variant spelling of *terdecies*
6. cui ... superstes – *superstes* is typically followed by the dative, here of *qui*: 'surviving her'
7. duo lustra – literally 'twice five years': a *lustrum* was a propitiatory sacrifice made once every five years

---

Hoc marmore EDMUNDO WALLER
MARIAEQ. ex secundis nuptiis cojugi
Pientissimis parentibus pientissime parentavit
EDMUNDUS Filius.
Honores bene merentibus extremos dedit
Quos ipse fugit
EL. W. I.F. H.G. ex testamento H.M.P. mense Julii 1700

Notes:

1. Hoc marmore – ablative
2. Edmundo, Mariae – dative case; *Mariaeq.* – abbreviation of *Mariaeque*
3. cojugi – misspelling of *conjugi,* dative
4. pientissimis parentibus – dative in agreement with *Edmundo & Mariae*
5. pientissime – adverb
6. parentavit – from *parento*, literally means 'offering a solemn sacrifice in honour of one's parents', from the Roman Parentalia festival honouring the dead, hence *Edmundus Filius* is the subject of this verb
7. merentibus – present participle of verb *mereo*, dative in agreement with *Edmundo & Mariae*, 'to those deserving'
8. fugit – literally 'fled from' or 'did not seek', presumably Edmund Jr. stipulated in his will that he should not have a grand tomb, rather the money should be spent on this one for his parents
9. EL. W. I.F. H.G – the executors of Edmund Jr.'s will, identified by John Safford, an authority on Waller's life, as Elizabeth Waller, John Fanshaw and Henry Gould

10. H.M.P. – *Hoc Monumentum Posuerunt* – literally 'they placed this
     monument'

Recommended reading:

J. Parker   ***Reading Latin Epitaphs***
                       Cressar Publications
An excellent handbook for every Latinist – full of examples like
those in this chapter, each with thorough explanations. There's
also a vocabulary list, selected abbreviations and some basic Latin
grammar.

ENGLISH TRANSLATIONS

CHAPTERS 9-15

Use these translations to check the accuracy of your own, always bearing in mind that no two translations will ever be word-for-word the same. I have striven to make my versions as close as possible to the original Latin, always preferring an inelegant but pedantically literal reading that makes the grammar clear to a more elegant one.

Chapter 9

A. SELECTIONS FROM THE VULGATE

1. *The Lord's Prayer*
Our father, you who are in the heavens: may your name be made holy. May your kingdom come. Let your will be done, on earth just as in heaven. Give to us today our daily bread. And release us from our debts, just as we release those who are indebted to us. And may you not lead us into temptation. But deliver us from evil. Amen.

2. *In the beginning ...*
In the beginning God created heaven and earth. But the earth was empty and void, and darkness was upon the face of the abyss: and the spirit of God was moving over the waters. And God said: Let there be light and the light was made. And God saw the light that it was good: and he divided the light from the darkness. And he called the light Day, and the darkness Night; it was done in the evening and the morning, the first day.

3. *The plague of frogs*
And God also said to Moses: approach the Pharaoh, and you will say to him: The Lord said these things: Release my people, so that they may sacrifice to me; but if you will have refused to release them, behold I will smite all your borders with frogs. And the river will produce frogs in abundance: which will rise up and enter your house,

and your bedroom and upon your blanket, and into the house of your servants, and against your people, and into your ovens, and into the leftovers of your food: And frogs will enter both upon you, and your people, and all your servants.

4. *And shepherds watched their flocks by night*
And there were shepherds in that same region watching and standing guard over their flock throughout the night watches. And Lo! An Angel of the Lord stood next to them, and the brightness of God shone round them, and they feared with great fear. And the Angel said to them: Do not be afraid, for Lo! I proclaim to you a great joy, which will be to all people: Because today a Saviour was born for you, he who is Christ the Lord, in the city of David. And this is a sign to you: You will find the infant wrapped in rags, and placed in a manger. And suddenly with the Angel a multitude of the heavenly host was created praising God, and saying: Glory in the highest to God, and on earth peace to men of good will.

B. VATICAN LATIN

1. '*Habemus Papam*'
'I announce to you a great joy. We have a Pope: the most eminent and reverend Master, Master Joseph Ratzinger, Cardinal of the Sacred Roman Church, who has chosen for himself the name Benedict the Sixteenth.'

Chapter 10

I. *Kyrie*

O Lord have mercy on us
O Christ have mercy on us
O Lord have mercy on us.

II. *Gloria*

Glory to God in the highest
And on earth peace to men of good will.
We praise you, we bless you,

We worship you, we glorify you,
We give thanks to you because of your great glory,
O Lord God, heavenly King,
God the all-powerful Father.
O Lord Jesus Christ, only-begotten Son;
O Lord God, Lamb of God, Son of the Father.
You who take away the sins of the world, have mercy on us,
You who take away the sins of the world, receive our prayer.
You who sit on the right hand of the Father, have mercy on us.
Because you alone are Holy, you alone are Lord, you alone are most high,
O Jesus Christ.
With the Holy Spirit in the glory of God the Father,
Amen.

III. *Credo*

I believe in one God, the all-powerful Father, maker of heaven and earth, of all things visible and invisible.
And in one Lord Jesus Christ, only-begotten Son of God.
And born from the Father before all the ages.
God of God, light of light, true God of true God.
Begotten, not made, of like substance with the Father, through whom all things were made.
He who for we men and for our salvation descended from the heavens.
And he was made flesh by the Holy Spirit from Mary the Virgin, and was made a man.
He was also crucified for us under Pontius Pilate, he suffered and was buried.
And he rose again on the third day, according to the Scriptures.
And he ascended into heaven, he sits at the right hand of the Father.
And he will come again with glory, to judge the living and the dead, whose reign will not end.
And in the Holy Spirit Lord, and giver of life, who proceeds from the Father and the Son.
Who together with the Father and the Son is worshipped and glorified, who spoke through the Prophets.
And in one holy, catholic and apostolic Church.

I confess one baptism for the remission of sins.
And I await the resurrection of the dead.
And the life of the world to come. Amen.

IV. *Sanctus*

Holy, Holy, Holy, Lord God of hosts;
Heaven and earth are full of your glory.
Hosanna in the highest.

V. *Benedictus*

Blessed is he who comes in the name of the Lord.
Hosanna in the highest.

VI. *Agnus Dei*

Lamb of God, who takes away the sins of the world, have mercy
on us.
Lamb of God, who takes away the sins of the world, give us peace.

Chapter 11

I. *Introit*

Grant to them eternal rest, O Lord,
and let perpetual light shine on them.
It befits you, O God, that a hymn of praise is sung in Sion,
and a vow will be returned to you in Jerusalem.
Hear my prayer, to you all flesh will come.

II. *Kyrie*

see Chapter 10

III. *Sequence*

(i) Dies iræ
Day of wrath, that day

Will dissolve the earth in ashes
As David and the Sibyl bear witness.

What dread there will be
When the Judge shall come
To judge all things strictly.

(ii) Tuba mirum
A trumpet spreading a wondrous sound
Through the graves of all regions
Will drive all before the throne.

Death will be astonished, and Nature
When Creation shall rise again
To answer to the Judge.

A book, written in, will be brought forth
In which is contained everything
From which the world will be judged.

When therefore the Judge will sit
Whatever is hidden will appear,
Nothing will remain unavenged.

What then am I, wretch, to say,
What advocate am I to ask to defend me,
When the just may hardly be secure?

(iii) Rex tremendae
King of fearful majesty,
Who freely saves the redeemed,
Save me, O fount of goodness.

(iv) Recordare
Remember, merciful Jesus,
Because I am the cause of your journey,
Do not forsake me on that day.

Seeking me you did sit down weary,

You redeemed me suffering on the cross,
Let not such toil be in vain.

Judge of vengeance justly
Grant forgiveness
Before the day of reckoning.

I groan like a guilty man,
My face blushes with guilt,
Spare a suppliant, O God.

You who absolved Mary [Magdalene]
And favourably heard the thief,
Also to me have given hope.

My prayers are not worthy,
But you who are merciful grant benignly
That I may not burn in everlasting fire.

Show me a place among your sheep
And separate me from the goats,
Standing me on your right.

(v) Confutatis
When the damned have been confounded
And sacrificed to the bitter flames,
Call me with the blessed.

A suppliant kneeling I beg,
My heart contrite as the dust,
Safeguard my end.

(vi) Lacrimosa
Mournful that day
When from the ashes shall rise
The guilty man to be judged.
Therefore spare him, O God.
O Merciful Jesus, Lord,
Grant them rest.

IV. *Offertory*

(i) Domine Jesu

O Lord, Jesus Christ, King of glory,
Deliver the souls of all the faithful departed
From the punishments of hell, and from the bottomless pit:
Deliver them from the lion's mouth,
Let not the infernal region swallow them up, nor let them fall into
  darkness,
But let St Michael the standard-bearer,
Lead them back into the holy light,
Which once you promised to Abraham
And his descendants.

(ii) Hostias

Sacrifices and prayers to you, O Lord,
Well-deserved we offer:
You receive them for the sake of those souls,
Whom today we commemorate:
Grant them, O Lord, to cross over from death into the life,
Which once you promised to Abraham
And his descendants.

V. *Sanctus* & VI. *Benedictus*

see Chapter 10

VII. *Agnus Dei*

Lamb of God, who takes away the sins of the world,
Grant them rest ...
Grant them everlasting rest.

VIII. *Communion*

Let eternal light shine on them, O Lord,
With your saints for ever,
Because you are merciful.
Grant them eternal rest, O Lord,

And let perpetual light shine on them,
With your saints for ever,
Because you are merciful.

Chapter 12

A. CHRISTMAS CAROLS

1. *Adeste fideles*
Be present, O faithful ones, joyful, exulting;
Come, come to Bethlehem
See the born King of angels
Come let us worship the Lord

God of God, Light of Light,
The girl's womb carries him;
True God, begotten not created:
Come let us worship the Lord

Let the choir of angels sing now songs of praise;
Let the courtiers of the heavens sing:
Glory to God in the highest!
Come let us worship the Lord.

Therefore you who are born on this very day,
O Jesus, may you have glory;
The word of the everlasting father made flesh.
Come let us worship the Lord.

2. *Personent hodie*
Let boyish voices ring out today,
praising joyously he who is born to us,
given by God on high,
and begotten from the virgin's womb.

He is born in the world, wrapped in swaddling clothes,
placed in a manger in a stable of animals,
Ruler of the heavens.
The prince of hell has lost the prize.

The three wise men came, they searched for the little infant,
They approached Bethlehem, (by) following the little star,
worshipping him,
offering to him gold, frankincense and myrrh.

Let all the (little) clerics, equally the boys,
sing like angels: you came to the world,
I pour out praises to you.
Therefore glory to God in the highest.

3. *Quem pastores laudavere*
He whom the shepherds praised,
to whom the angels said:
'Do not be afraid:
the King of Glory is born!'

The magi travelled towards him,
carrying gold, frankincense and myrrh;
they offered these things sincerely
to the Lion of victory;

To Christ the King, to the Son of God,
given to us through Mary,
let 'Praise, honour and glory!' right worthily resound!

B. HYMNS

1. *Ave Maria*
Hail Mary, full of grace, the Lord is with you,
you are blessed among women,
and Jesus, the fruit of your womb, is blessed.
Holy Mary, Mother of God,
speak on behalf of we sinners, now,
and in the hour of our death,
Amen.

2. *Stabat mater*
The sorrowful Mother was standing,

next to the cross weeping,
while the Son was hanging.

Whose soul groaning,
saddening and grieving,
The sword pierced through.

O how sad and desponding
Was that blessed
Mother of the only-begotten.

She was mourning and grieving,
and trembling while watching
the punishments of her famous son.

Is there any man who would not weep
if he saw the Mother of Christ
in such distress?

Who would not be sad,
contemplating the Devoted Mother
grieving with the Son?
For the sins of His race
she saw Jesus in torments,
and subjected to the whips.

She saw her sweet son
dying forsaken
while he let loose his spirit.

Oh Mother, fount of love,
make me feel the power of your sorrow,
so that I may mourn with you.

Grant that my heart may glow
in the loving of Christ God,
so that I may greatly please him.
Holy Mother, may you do that,

drive the wounds of the crucified
strongly through my heart.

Divide with me the wounds
of your wounded son
who so deigned to suffer for me.

Make me truly weep with you
feel the pain of the crucifixion
while I am alive.

I long to stand next to the cross with you,
to join willingly with you
in lamentation.
admirable Virgin of virgins,
may you not be severe towards me,
make me grieve with you.

Grant that I may carry the death of Christ,
make me share in his suffering,
and reflect upon his wounds.
Make me wounded with his wounds,
steeped in this cross
on account of the Son.

When I am burnt and set on fire
through you, O Virgin, may I be defended
on the day of judgement.

Make me guarded by the cross,
fortified by the death of Christ,
cherished by His grace.

When my body will die,
grant that the glory of paradise
may be given to my soul.
Amen.

Chapter 13

1. *Carmina Burana: O Fortuna*
O Fortune,
just like the moon
variable in state,
always waxing
or waning;
detestable life
now hardens
and then softens
the mind's understanding as a joke;
it melts poverty,
power
as [the sun melts] ice.

O monstrous Fate
and empty,
you are a whirling wheel,
an evil condition,
a vain safety
always dissolving,
concealed
and veiled
you will also assail me
now through the game
of your villainy
I bear my naked back.

Fate of safety
and virtue
opposed to me;
always in servitude
there is affection
and its absence.
In this hour
without delay
touch the beat in my heart;
because through Fate

Fortune has overthrown the strong
all mourn with me now.

2. *Gaudeamus igitur*
Let us rejoice therefore,
While we are young;
After a pleasant youth
After a troublesome old age
The earth will have us.

Our life is brief,
It will be finished shortly;
Death comes quickly,
Snatches us away cruelly;
No one is spared.

Where are they who before us
Were in the world?
Go to the upper world,
Cross over to the underworld,
If you wish to see them.

Let the academy live on,
Let the professors live on,
Let each male student live on,
Let each female student live on;
Let them always be in their prime.

And let the State live on
And he who rules it,
Let our city live on,
And the charity of benefactors,
Which protects us here.

Let all young women live on,
Easy, beautiful,
And let mature women live on,
Tender, amiable
Good, laborious.

Let sadness perish,
Let haters perish,
Let the devil perish
Whoever is against our school,
And mocks at it.

Who of the university
Has gathered today?
They have assembled from afar,
They came up immediately
Jointly into the forum.

Let our society live on,
Let the scholarly live on!
Let one truth be strengthened,
Let our fraternity flourish,
The prosperity of our homeland.

Let our Alma Mater flourish,
Which educated us;
[Which has] gathered together
Dear ones and comrades,
Scattered in remote regions.

Chapter 14

A. FUNERARY INSCRIPTIONS

1. *Epitaph for a Young Boy*
The freedman Optatus lived six years eight months ...
O Optatus, may the earth rest lightly upon you

2. *Roman Funerary Marker*
The bones
Of Pomponia Platura
Gaius's freedwoman

3. *Tombstone of Flavia Victorinae*
To the memory of

Flavia Victorina
Titus Tammonius Victor
Her Husband
Set this up

4. *Gravestone of Caecilius Avitus*
To the spirits of the departed
Caecilius Avitus, from Emerita Augusta
Optio of the 20th Legion
Valeria Victorious, of 15 years' service
Lived 34 years
His heir saw to this being made

B. ALTARS

1. *Mithraic Altar from Vindobala*
To the unconquered god
Mithras Publius Aelius
Flavinus, Prefect,
Fulfilled his vow gladly, willingly, deservedly

2. *Mithraic Altar from Brocolitia*
Sacred to the Unconquered God Mithras
Aulus Cluentius
Habitus, Prefect
Of the First Cohort
Of Batavians
Of the Ultinian Voting-Tribe
From Colonia Septimia Aurelia Larinum
Fulfilled his vow willingly and deservedly

3. *Altar from Verocovicium*
To Jupiter Best and Greatest
And to the God Cocidius
And to the Genius of this place
The soldiers of the Second Legion Augusta
While on garrison duty
Fulfilled their vow willingly and deservedly

C. MONUMENTAL INSCRIPTIONS

1. *The Pantheon, Rome*
Marcus Agrippa, son of Lucius, consul three times, built (it)

2. *The Arch of Titus, Rome*
The Senate and People of Rome to the deified Titus Vespasian, Augustus, son of the deified Vespasian

3. *Slab from Bremenium*
A detachment
Of the Twentieth Legion Valeria Victorious
Built this

4. *Verulamium*
To the emperor Titus Caesar Vespasian Augustus, son of the deified Vespasian
Chief Priest, holder of the Tribunician power nine times, saluted Emperor fifteen times, Consul seven times, designated Consul for an eighth time, Censor, Father of his country
And to Caesar Domitian, son of the deified Vespasian, Consul six times, designated Consul for a seventh time
Leader of the youth and of all the priestly colleges
The colony of Verulamium while Gnaeus Julius Agricola was Legate of Augustus with the power of a Praetor, having furnished this basilica, [dedicate it].

Chapter 15

A. FAMOUS LATIN EPITAPHS

1. *Samuel Johnson, Poets' Corner, Westminster Abbey*
Samuel Johnson, Doctor of Laws
Died on the 13th day of December
In the year of our Lord
1784
Aged 75

2. Jonathan Swift, St Patrick's Cathedral
Here is laid the body of
Jonathan Swift, Doctor of Sacrosanct Theology,
Of this cathedral church
Dean
Where savage indignation
Can no longer tear his heart.
Go, traveller,
And imitate, if you can,
To the best of his ability a strenuous
Defender of liberty

He died on the 19th day of the month of October
In the year of our Lord 1745 Aged 78

3. Oliver Goldsmith, Poets' Corner, Westminster Abbey
The love of his companions,
The fidelity of his friends,
And the veneration of his readers has
By this monument honoured the memory of Oliver Goldsmith
Poet, Natural Philosopher, Historian,
Who scarcely any style of writing
Did not touch
Nothing that he touched he did not adorn
Whether laughs were to be stirred
Or tears,
A powerful yet mild ruler of the passions
In genius sublime, vivid, versatile,
In style lofty, polished, elegant.
He was born in Ireland in the Parish of Ferney, County of Longford
In a place called Pallas
On the 29th Nov 1731 (actually 1728),
Educated at the University of Dublin,
He died in London,
4th April 1774

4. Christopher Wren, St Paul's Cathedral
Beneath lies buried
The founder of this church and city

Christopher Wren
Who lived more than 90 years
Not for himself but for the public good
Reader, if you seek his monument
Look around

He died on 25th February in the year 1723 Aged 91

B. LOCAL LATIN EPITAPHS

1. *St Mary's Church, Amersham*
To God
Greatest and best.
In pious memory of
Frederick Edward
Tyrwhitt Drake,
Priest,
Born 27th September 1828,
Died 29th August, 1909,

Of Montague William
Tyrwhitt Drake,
Born 20th January 1830,
Died 10th March 1908,

[And] of William Henry
Tyrwhitt Drake,
Born 6th July 1835,
Died 13th April 1898.

George Tyrwhitt Drake
– died 1840 –
And Jane Halsey his wife
– died 1864 –
begot these three sons

May Jesus have mercy on their souls (see note)

2. *Tomb of Edmund Waller*

Hark! Traveller, you see the tomb of Edmund Waller,

A poet of great renown and also remarkable

Among the most distinguished men for his ancestral wealth; he
dedicated himself to the muses and to his country.

Not yet in his eighteenth year during the difficulties of a protracted
rule,

Sent from the town of Amersham he held a seat.

This was the course of his life: nor as an old man did he neglect
the burden

[or: 'lack respect'] and lived always

Dear to the people, a favourite among Princes, admired by all.

Here is buried under this same tomb,

Celebrated for rare virtue and many children

His wife MARIA from the family of Bressy,

with her dearest husband EDMUND WALLER,

Whom three times and ten she made a happy father

With five sons and eight daughters

Which she gave to this world, and then returned into heaven

Here lies that much of Edmund Waller which yielded to death

He who among the poets of his time was easily the foremost

The young man deserved that Laurel crown

Which the octogenarian by no means renounced

To him his native language owes, you may believe it,

If the muses should leave off in Greek and Latin

They would be pleased to speak in English

Edmund Waller, to whom this marble is sacred

Had Coleshill as the place of his birth, Cambridge as his place of
study

Robert as his father and a mother from the Hampden family

He began to live on the 3rd of March 1605

His first wife was Anna, only daughter and heir of Edward Banks

From his first wife he was made a father twice; from the second
thirteen times

Whom he also survived ten years. He died on 21st October 1687

With this marble the son Edmund

Most affectionately offers a solemn memorial to his most beloved parents, Edmund Waller and Maria, wife from his second marriage.

He gives final honours which he himself shunned

To those well deserving

According to his will, Elizabeth Waller, John Fanshaw [and] Henry Gould set up this monument in the month of July 1700.

A BRIEF GUIDE TO LATIN (AND ENGLISH!) GRAMMAR

(1) Why Latin grammar?

Nowadays modern foreign languages are taught conversationally: people want to speak the language, obviously. But in days gone by schoolchildren learned, say, French in order to read great French literature, not to order a baguette at the local café, and hence they required a more thorough grounding in the structure of the language. The teaching of Latin remains resolutely old-fashioned in this respect, because (a) its principal aim is still to enable students to read Latin literature and (b) the chances of acquiring Latin conversationally are extremely limited (unless you happen to live in the Vatican).

Latin is also an *inflected* language, which means that almost all Latin words change their form (usually their endings) depending on their role in a sentence or clause: so if you don't understand the grammatical role of a particular form of a Latin word you won't be able to translate it.

Let's look a little more closely at inflection. In English, the grammatical function of a word usually depends on its position within a sentence, e.g.

* The boy loves the girl

Here 'boy' is the subject of the verb 'loves', which simply means that he is the person doing the action of the verb, while 'girl' is the direct object: she is the person on the receiving end of the action, directly in the firing line if you will. In Latin the same sentence looks like this:

* puer puellam amat

Puer ('boy') is the subject, *amat* ('he loves') is the verb and *puellam* ('girl') is the direct object. Note that in Latin the verb usually comes at the end of the sentence or clause; note also the absence of the definite article 'the'. Contrast with:

- The girl loves the boy

In English, change of word order changes the <u>meaning</u>. Now it's the girl doing the loving and the boy receiving it. But in Latin, change the word order and <u>the meaning does not change</u>:

puellam puer amat

This still means 'The boy loves the girl'. Why? Because all three Latin words in this sentence are *inflected*, and it is this inflection that determines their meaning, not their position relative to each other. In this second Latin sentence all we have changed is the emphasis: 'It is this girl whom the boy loves.'

Changing the voice of the first sentence from active to passive we get:

The girl is loved by the boy   Puella a puero amatur

Where the girl who was the object (accusative *puellam*) of the first sentence now becomes the subject (nominative *puella*), and the boy who was the subject (nominative *puer*) now becomes what is known as the agent (the 'doer' of the verb), expressed in Latin by the ablative case (*puero*) prefixed by the preposition *a(b)*. Note how the verb ending has changed from *-t* (active: 'loves') to *-tur* (passive: 'is loved')

Inflection isn't entirely foreign to English:

•	*boy*	*(singular)*	*boys*	*(plural)*
•	*I*	*(subject)*	*me*	*(object)*
•	*(s)he*	*(subject)*	*her/him*	*(object)*
•	*who*	*(subject)*	*whom*	*(object)*
•	*does*	*(present tense)*	*did*	*(past tense)*

(2) Verbs and Nouns

Latin verbs are conventionally grouped into one of five conjugations. To conjugate a verb is to list the inflected forms of a verb in order of persons. Where English uses personal pronouns ('I', 'You', 'We' etc.), Latin verbs use different word endings instead: present tense active *-o, -s, -t, -mus, -tis, -nt*. But it's no more complicated than English: in English, we typically have two parts to a verb, i.e. the word itself plus the personal pronoun (e.g. 'I walk, 'They walk'); while the Latin verb still has two components: (a) the **stem**, which is the main body of the word and carries its meaning, plus (b) the **ending**, which tells us who is doing the action of the verb.

A typical verb conjugation looks like this:

amo, amare (stem *ama-*) – 'I love', 'I like' (present tense indicative active)

Person	Singular	English	Endings
1st	amo	I love, am loving, do love	-o
2nd	amas	You love, are loving, do love	-s
3rd	amat	He, she, it loves, is loving, does love	-t
	Plural		
1st	amamus	We love, are loving, do love	-mus
2nd	amatis	You love, are loving, do love	-tis
3rd	amant	They love, are loving, do love	-nt

Nouns are names, not just of specific people ('Caesar') or things ('The Senate'), but also of classes ('Dogs', 'Men') and concepts ('Courage', 'Honour'). Latin nouns are declined according to a fixed list of cases. These cases define the grammatical function of the noun in a sentence or clause – they indicate its relationship to the verb, whether it is subject or object, or if it is playing a different role, such as part of a prepositional phrase.

A typical noun declension looks like this:

femina, feminae (English 'feminine') – 'woman', 'a woman', 'the woman'

Case	Singular	English	Endings
Nominative	femina	woman (subject)	-a
Accusative	feminam	woman (direct object)	-am
Genitive	feminae	of a woman (possessive)	-ae
Dative	feminae	to, for a woman (indirect object)	-ae
Ablative	femina	by, with, from a woman	-a
	Plural		
Nominative	feminae	women (subject)	-ae
Accusative	feminas	women (direct object)	-as
Genitive	feminarum	of women (possessive)	-arum
Dative	feminis	to, for women (indirect object)	-is
Ablative	feminis	by, with, from women	-is

(3) A Grammar Glossary

A brief explanation of the key grammatical terms used in this book:

Ablative Case	generally translated into English as 'with...', 'from...' or 'by ...'; also used with many prepositions
Accusative Case	the Direct Object of a verb, e.g. 'ball' in 'John kicks the <u>ball</u>'; also used with some prepositions
Active Voice	the voice in which the Subject (Nominative case) of the verb is the one doing the action, e.g. '<u>John</u> kicks the ball'. *cf.* Passive Voice
Adjective	describes a noun or pronoun
Adverb	shows how the action of a verb is carried out
Agreement	an adjective is said to agree with the noun it describes when it is the same gender, number and case as that noun
Case	the form of the noun, pronoun or adjective which defines its use in a sentence or clause

Comparative	an adjective or adverb that is '-er' in English, e.g. 'longer', 'better'
Conjugation	all the different parts of a verb in order of persons
Conjunction	a linking word, e.g. 'and', 'but'
Dative Case	the Indirect Object of a verb, often translated by 'to...' or 'for...', expressing that the person in the dative is usually either a gainer or loser by the action; also the object of many Latin intransitive verbs
Declension	the list of all the cases of a noun, pronoun or adjective
Deponent Participles	the perfect (past) participle of a deponent verb is active in meaning, not passive, e.g. *mortuus* = 'died'
Deponent Verb	a verb that conjugates like a passive but is active in meaning
Future Participle	the verb as an adjective in the future, 'about to ...', 'on the point of ...'
Future Perfect Tense	the tense of action completed in the future, e.g. 'I will have done'
Future Tense	the tense of an action in the future
Gender	masculine, feminine or neuter – does not refer to actual sex but to conventional classifications of words into grammatical genders
Genitive Case	denotes possession and other qualities expressed by the English preposition 'of'
Gerund	the verb when acting as a noun (English '-ing' words)
Gerundive	the verb when acting as a passive adjective, 'to be –ed'
Imperative	the mood of a verb expressing a command
Imperfect Tense	the past tense of ongoing action, 'I was –ing'
Impersonal Verbs	verbs with no subject, e.g. 'It's raining'
Indicative	the mood of a verb that states the action as a fact
Infinitive	the form of a verb that doesn't have a tense e.g. 'to love', 'to walk', 'to be'
Inflection	the change in form, usually the endings, of Latin words

Interjection
an exclamation!

Intransitive Verbs
verbs are said to be intransitive when they don't take a direct object in the accusative case. Many have an indirect object in the dative instead. English examples include verbs of motion, e.g. 'go' as in 'I go to the park'. *cf.* Transitive Verbs

Irregular Verbs
those verbs (e.g. *sum*) that do not conjugate regularly

Locative Case
denotes the place where something is happening, e.g. *domi* = 'at home'

Mood
the mood of a verb can be indicative, subjunctive or imperative

Nominative Case
denotes the Subject of a verb in a sentence or clause, e.g. 'John' in '<u>John</u> kicks the ball'

Noun
a name of a person, place, thing or abstraction

Number
singular or plural

Participles
the form of a verb when it is used as an adjective: in Latin they can be Perfect (past), Present or Future

Passive Voice
in the Passive, the Subject of the verb is having the action done to him/her/it, e.g. 'The ball is kicked by John', and the 'doer' of the verb goes into the Latin ablative case (English 'by ...'). *cf.* Active Voice

Perfect Participle Passive
the verb as an adjective in the perfect tense, passive in meaning, 'having been -ed'

Perfect tense
the past tense of action that has been completed

Person
'I/we' (first person), 'you' (both singular & plural, second person), 'he, she, it, they' (third person)

Pluperfect Tense
the past tense of action further back than the perfect, 'I had –ed'. An English example: 'After <u>I had put on</u> my pyjamas, I went to bed'

Possessive Adjectives
'my', 'your', 'our', 'his', 'her', 'their'

Preposition
e.g. 'in', 'by', 'with', 'from' – followed in Latin by either the accusative or ablative cases

Present Participle
the verb as an adjective in the present, 'while –ing'

Present Tense
the tense of current or ongoing action

Principal Parts	the four key parts of a verb necessary to form all its conjugations
Pronoun	used in place of a noun, e.g. 'he', 'she', 'it'
Relative Pronoun	the relative pronouns *qui* (masculine), *quae* (feminine), *quod* (neuter) introduce a clause that says 'who ...' or 'which ...'; it is much more common in Latin than in English
Subjunctive	the mood of a verb that expresses wishes, possibilities or indirect commands
Superlative	an adjective or adverb that is '-est' in English, e.g. 'longest', 'best'
Tense	the time at which the action of a verb takes place
Transitive Verbs	verbs that regularly take a direct object in the accusative case. *cf.* Intransitive Verbs
Verb	a word that indicates action or a state of being
Vocative Case	used when addressing someone: *Domine* = 'O Lord'
Voice	a verb is either active or passive voice *(q.v.)*

INDEX